CALL YOURSELF
A SPURS FAN?

THE ULTIMATE
TOTTENHAM
HOTSPUR
QUIZ BOOK

DEDICATION

This book is for my son Dan and our mutual friend Darrell De Souza. Between them they have clocked up many hours at White Hart Lane over many years.

It's also to the memory of Dave Mackay who was one hell of a player.

ACKNOWLEDGEMENTS

Many thanks to my friend of more years than I care to remember, John Shaw, for his assistance in this project.

RACING POST

CALL YOURSELF
A SPURS FAN?

THE ULTIMATE
TOTTENHAM HOTSPUR
QUIZ BOOK

MART MATTHEWS

First published by Pitch Publishing on behalf of Racing Post, 2021

Pitch Publishing
A2 Yeoman Gate
Yeoman Way
Worthing
Sussex
BN13 3QZ

www.pitchpublishing.co.uk
info@pitchpublishing.co.uk
www.racingpost.com/shop

A CIP catalogue record is available for this book
from the British Library.

ISBN 9781839500763

Typesetting and origination by Pitch Publishing

Printed and bound in India by Replika Press Pvt. Ltd.

CONTENTS

INTRODUCTION

Hello Spurs fans and welcome to what I hope is the most comprehensive quiz on your club available.

A word or two on the League Cup is required here. Since its inception in the 1960/61 season, it has had several sponsors, among them five companies involved with drinks. Here's an early question for you. Who are they? To me it has always been the League Cup whatever transient sponsor it has at any moment in time. It is a tedious task to look up who is sponsoring it at any particular time, and therefore in this quiz it will be known as 'the League Cup'.

My choice of 12 players in the 'Super Spurs' section will probably differ here and there from yours, but if it provokes a few disagreements it's all to the good.

I hope you enjoy it.

QUIZ No. 1

ACROSS THE CAPITAL

All these players left White Hart Lane and moved to another London club. You are given the number of league games each of them played for Spurs and the year they left. Which clubs did they join?

1. Les Allen – 119 Games – 1965

2. Dean Austin – 124 Games – 1997

3. Johnny Brooks – 166 Games – 1960

4. Ralph Coates – 188 Games – 1978

5. Billy Cook – 63 Games – 1931

6. Terry Dyson – 184 Games – 1965

7. Don McAllister – 172 Games – 1981

8. Stuart Nethercott – 54 Games – 1997

9. Jimmy Robertson – 157 Games – 1969

10. Mitchell Thomas – 157 Games – 1991

QUIZ No. 2

ANYTHING GOES – PART 1

1. Martin Jol, Spurs manager between 2004 and 2007, played football in England as a wing-half with which two Midlands clubs?

2. A player in Spurs' double-winning team of 1960/61 shares a surname with a member of Arsenal's double-winning team of 1997/98. What is that surname?

3. Recent Spurs manager Mauricio Pochettino kept what in his office to ward off negative energy? I'm at an age when any form of energy is welcome, and the negative variety is often preferable!

4. He came on once for Spurs as a substitute before leaving for Middlesbrough in 1972, becoming perhaps the greatest player to slip through the club's fingers. Who was he?

5. When Spurs beat Atletico Madrid 5-1 to win the European Cup Winners' Cup in 1963, one of their Spanish opponents had the same surname as one of the Spurs players. What was that unlikely surname?

6. Scott Houghton is a marginal figure in Spurs' history. He never started a game, coming on as a substitute ten times in total. However, on 16 November 1991 he got two goals for the club, matching Gary Lineker's contribution in a 4-1 win against Luton Town at White Hart Lane. Those were his only Spurs goals and he later joined the club he scored them against. What transpired that afternoon, for the first time since 17 December 1969 against Everton, that made the game memorable?

7. Spurs signed Peter Murphy from Coventry City in 1950 and he played 38 times for the club, scoring 14 goals before moving to Birmingham City in 1952. While there he played in the 1956 Cup Final and was involved in what incident?

8. Which Spurs player, who shares his surname with a prime minister, came to the club from Wimbledon in 2000, making 36 appearances before moving on to Leicester City in 2003?

9. On 22 July 1995, Spurs suffered their heaviest defeat when they lost 8-0 to Cologne in what competition?

10. A crowd of just short of 13,000 turned up at Home Park, Plymouth, in early December 1961 to watch a reserve game. Why?

QUIZ No. 3

ANYTHING GOES - PART 2

1. Pat Jennings played his last game for Spurs on 14 May 1977 at White Hart Lane. Strangely enough, the game ended with the same result as an earlier post-war Spurs FA Cup Final. Who did Spurs play in his final game and what was the score?

2. When Spurs did the 'double' in 1960/61 it posed a problem for the Charity Shield, the traditional curtain raiser to the new season, because normally the league champions played the FA Cup winners, but Spurs couldn't play themselves. Who did they play?

3. In which tournament in 1970 did Spurs beat Dunfermline and lose to Motherwell over two legs?

4. Three post-war Spurs managers have been followed in that role by a man whose surname began with the same letter as the departing manager. Which six managers are involved here?

5. When Tottenham Hotspur began their league residency at Wembley Stadium on 20 August 2017 against Chelsea, who scored their first goal in that ground?

6. On the opening day of the 2018/19 season, Spurs made the long journey to Newcastle and came away with a 2-1 win. Their first goal of that season was deemed by the technology to have crossed the line by 9mm. Who scored it?

7. In their first season in the Football League in 1908, the club Spurs met on both Christmas Day and Boxing Day sound like something you wouldn't want to eat because it's been hanging around for a while! Who were they?

8. When Spurs paid Newcastle £2 million for Paul Gascoigne in the summer of 1988, he made his debut for the club against which opponents?

9. Who is the odd man out of the following four players and why? Danny Blanchflower, Glenn Hoddle, Gary Lineker and Dimitar Berbatov.

10. In the mid-1980s, under the chairmanship of Irving Scholar, what business decision did Spurs take that made them unique among Football League clubs?

QUIZ No. 4

BIRTHPLACES

1. In which country was Nayim 'from the halfway line' born?

2. Sid Tickridge, Vic Groves, Clive Allen and Paul Miller were all born in an area of London that shares its name with a post-war England goalkeeper. Where were they born?

3. Alf Ramsey, Les Allen, and Terry Venables played over 500 games for Spurs between them and all shared the same birth place. What was it?

4. Tom Huddlestone and Jermaine Jenas were born in the same English city, and Martin Chivers and Darren Anderton also shared a birthplace about 160 miles south of that first city. Which two cities are involved here?

5. Tottenham's Eric Dier was born in the same town as Brian Jones of the Rolling Stones. Where?

6. The two Kyle's, Naughton and Walker, were born within two years of each other in the same city. Which one?

7. Micky Hazard, Andy Sinton, Terry Fenwick and Chris Armstrong all came from the same part of England. Which?

8. Spurs goalkeeper Paulo Gazzaniga was born in Argentina but you could be forgiven for thinking he was born in Ireland. Why?

9. Len Duquemin scored goals galore for Spurs in the late 1940s and early 1950s. Where did he hail from?

10. Les Ferdinand was born in a part of London celebrated by Van Morrison in his song 'Slim Slow Slider' from the album *Astral Weeks*. Where was Les born?

QUIZ No. 5

THE CHELSEA CONNECTION

1. Which two members of the double-winning side of 1960/61 had previously played for Chelsea?

2. Who is the only player to score over 120 goals for both clubs?

3. On 6 March 1982, he scored one of the goals at Stamford Bridge that helped Spurs beat Chelsea 3-2 in the FA Cup sixth round. In 1985 he crossed London to join them. Who was he?

4. Two men who played for Chelsea in the 1960s both went on to manage Spurs. Who were they?

5. Which striker did Spurs sign from Chelsea in 1991 who played 78 times for the club before his move to Glasgow Rangers in 1994?

6. Only two men in this century have managed both Spurs and Chelsea. Who are they?

7. This popular central defender started exactly 200 league games for Spurs between 1980 and 1986 and, after a short sojourn with Glasgow Rangers, joined Chelsea in 1988. Who was he?

8. Which Spurs player from the 1950s and 1960s went on to manage Chelsea in the 1970s?

9. Only one man in the post-war era has played for and managed both Chelsea and Spurs. Who is he?

10. A quality midfielder who could score goals as well, this Uruguayan played for Chelsea between 1997 and 2001 and then went to Spurs until 2004. Who was he?

QUIZ No. 6

CHRISTMAS CRACKERS

1. This sounds incredible, but it's true. Between 1898 and 1907, in the Southern League, Spurs played the same team on the same ground on ten successive Boxing Days. Who were their opponents and what was the venue?

2. On Boxing day of 1912, a player who scored 74 goals in 159 league games for Spurs got a hat-trick at White Hart Lane in a 4-0 win over Manchester City. Who was he?

3. Two years later, on Boxing Day, Bert Bliss, a great goalscorer with a name to match, lit up White Hart Lane by scoring four times in a 6-1 win over which Yorkshire club?

4. Whatever method was used to allocate Christmas matches at this time, it was kind to Spurs in 1931 by pairing them with another London club. Spurs lost 1-0 away on Christmas Day, but beat the same team 5-2 the following day when free-scoring Yorkshireman George Hunt grabbed a hat-trick. Which London club did they play over Christmas that year?

5. In 1952 Spurs drew the short straw again and had to travel to Middlesbrough on 27 December, a match they won 4-0. On Christmas Day itself they had already hammered that club 7-1 at White Hart Lane. Which local lad scored four of the seven, those four ending up being crucial to his final total of 103 league goals for Spurs?

6. If the team that Spurs beat 6-0 at White Hart Lane on Christmas Day 1956 thought that was the end of their troubles on that ground they were in for a shock two years later when they lost by the same margin but a different score line in a match that has gone down in Spurs folklore. Who were they?

7. The team that took Spurs' league crown in 1961/62 were already in decline by Boxing Day of 1962 when they were put to the sword 5-0 at White Hart Lane, with Jimmy Greaves helping himself to three of them. Who were they?

8. On Boxing Day of 1963 there were a record 66 goals scored in the ten top-flight games. Spurs played their part by sharing eight goals away to which Midlands club?

9. The next time Spurs were involved in a 4-4 draw on Boxing Day was in 1980 at White Hart Lane against Southampton, who were also the visitors at Wembley on Boxing Day 2017, when which Spurs player scored a hat-trick in a 5-2 win?

10. Spurs produced a torrent of goals at Christmas in 2018, scoring 11 times in their two games. It began with an away win at Everton on 23 December and concluded with victory over Bournemouth at White Hart Lane on Boxing Day. What were the two score lines?

QUIZ No. 7

'COME ON YOU SPURS' - FANS

1. 'Someone like you' could be a Spurs fan, according to this singer, who already is! Who is she?

2. The World Snooker champion of 2002 was a big Spurs fan. Who was he?

3. Fans of EastEnders will know the Spurs fan who played Ricky Butcher. Do you?

4. A massive Spurs fan was responsible for training Sixties Icon to win the 2006 St. Leger, the only time it was run at York. Who was he?

5. No wonder he always looked depressed and pissed off in *Wallander*, it turns out he was a Spurs fan. Which actor played the part?

6. The script of *Til Death Us Do Part* required Alf Garnett to be a West Ham fan, but in real life the actor who played him was to be found at White Hart Lane rather than Upton Park. Who was he?

7. Widely considered to be one of Britain's greatest comedians, he once did a sketch that featured a Spurs v Norwich game, and certainly earned his spurs when he was 'duffed up', in the terminology of the time, outside Old Trafford. Who was he?

8. A fan, as well as an insightful observer of the club, he wrote *The Glory Game*, a behind-the-scenes look at life at White Hart Lane in the 1970s. Who was he?

9. You have to be a bit philosophical to be a Spurs supporter, and that posed few problems for this man who was one of Britain's foremost philosophers of the 20th century. Who was he?

10. Who was the Spurs fan responsible for *Spurred on TV* who ended each show with 'Come on you Spurs!'?

QUIZ No. 8

CRYPTIC SCORERS AGAINST ARSENAL

A goal against Arsenal is always welcome. You are given a cryptic clue and the decade in which they scored. Can you identify the players?

1. English forest – 1990s

2. Legendary trumpet player – 1990s

3. Biblical doubter – 1980s

4. Nut – 1980s

5. Murdered king in Macbeth – 1970s

6. Big hitting English cricketer – 1950s

7. Jelly makers – 1970s

8. Lawbreakers – 1980s

9. Stoke City owners – 1970s

10. Best avoided on a golf course – 1980s

QUIZ No. 9

CRYPTIC SPURS

You are given the dates they played for Spurs and a cryptic clue in each case. Can you identify the players?

1. In a Western, the Sheriff is usually left with the unenviable task of assembling one of these to go after the outlaws. (1963–66)

2. What ducks do. (1985–89)

3. Dwelling place and football club. (1978–83)

4. An earlier version changed his name on the road to Damascus, but this one kept his. (1960–68)

5. He remained unspoilt by his success, like the boy next door. (1970–77)

6. The one in the centre of three unmarried girls. (1907–20)

7. The only member of the double-winning team gathering dust. (1954–65)

8. Small town on the north Norfolk coast. (1992–97 and 2001–03)

9. Shares a surname with a great jazz guitarist and something that happens hundreds of times in a game. (1907–08)

10. Two for the price of one to finish! A country and a capital city that begin with the same letter. (1966–75 and 1990–2000)

QUIZ No. 10

DOUBLE DIAMONDS

For those of you old enough to remember the TV advert for this beer, it was supposed to work wonders. How appropriate, because the 1960/61 team did just that. If you were a Spurs fan from that era, or just a football lover, the 11 names roll off the tongue like a mantra. Brown, Baker, Henry, Blanchflower, Norman, Mackay, Jones, White, Smith, Allen, Dyson. I have 11 stairs in my house and still use it in the dark to know when I've safely reached the bottom! Here are ten questions about that remarkable team.

1. When Spurs won the league ten years before, in 1951, they clinched the title with a home win over the same side that they beat at White Hart Lane to win the 1961 title. Who were they?

2. Only one of the outfield players failed to score during the 42-match league programme. Who was he?

3. Four Spurs players appeared in every league game and the others missed few matches. Who, due to injury, could only turn out 29 times in the league that season?

4. Spurs started the season with 11 straight wins. Which club broke the sequence by holding them to a 1-1 draw at White Hart Lane on 10 October 1960?

5. Consistency was the key in the FA Cup as well, ten of the 11 playing in all seven cup ties. Which team did they beat on the way to Wembley that they had defeated the previous year at the same stage of the competition?

6. In doing the league and cup double, their achievement was special because no club had done it in the 20th century where far more games had to be played to achieve it. Which two clubs had done it in the previous century?

7. Growing up in Malton, a Yorkshire horse-racing town, which member of that team started out with hopes of following in his father's footsteps by becoming a jockey?

8. There were three Scots in the side. Dave Mackay and John White were born in Musselburgh, but Bill Brown came from the place known for 'smokies'. Where was he born?

9. Two Spurs players scored hat-tricks in the league and together they remind you of a 1970s Western TV series. Who are they?

10. Twice during the season Spurs scored six times in a league game. The two beaten clubs were from the same city. Which one?

QUIZ No. 11

ENGLAND CRICKET CAPTAINS

You may wonder what a section on England cricket captains is doing in a Spurs quiz book. However, Spurs did start out when boys from the Hotspur Cricket Club decided to try football in 1882 and, although it is hard to believe, 25 England cricket captains share a surname with a Spurs player. The post-war number is 11 and from those I've chosen ten.

1. Mike Atherton

2. Mike Brearley

3. Brian Close

4. Alastair Cook

5. David Gower

6. Len Hutton

7. Ray Illingworth

8. M. J. K. Smith

9. Alec Stewart

10. Bob Willis

A player with each of those surnames has played for Spurs. Can you rewrite the first name in each case to produce the Spurs player?

QUIZ No. 12

FA CUP FINALS - 1960s

1. Who was the only man to play for Spurs in the 1961, 1962 and 1967 FA Cup finals?

2. In those three FA Cup finals against Leicester City, Burnley and Chelsea, the opposing goalkeepers' names all began with the same letter. Who were they?

3. Who was the only Spurs player to score in more than one of those three finals?

4. The Spurs full-backs in the 1967 FA Cup Final had surnames that began with the same letter. Who were they?

5. When Spurs beat Leicester City in the 1961 final, they completed the first 'double' of the 20th century. Which player on the Leicester side that day would know that feeling himself ten years later?

6. If Spurs had used their substitute in 1967 against Chelsea a second player besides the answer to question one would have played in all three 1960s finals. Who?

7. Which two men who won an FA Cup winner's medal with Spurs in 1967 later played in an FA Cup Final for different clubs?

8. Which four players, two from each side, in the 1967 final between Spurs and Chelsea later joined Arsenal?

9. In the 1961 final between Spurs and Leicester City one player from each side shared a surname. What was it?

10. In the FA Cup Final against Leicester City, which Spurs player scored their second goal and with which part of his anatomy?

QUIZ No. 13

THE FA CUP FINALS OF
1901, 1921, 1981, 1982, 1987 AND 1991

1. When Spurs won the FA Cup for the first time in 1901 with a 3-1 replay win over Sheffield United, their goals were scored by three players, two of whom shared their surnames with post-war prime ministers, while the third shared his with a post-war leader of the opposition. Who were the three?

2. Who is the only Spurs player to score more than once in a post-war FA Cup Final or replay?

3. Who is the only man to score against Spurs in a post-war FA Cup Final and later to go on to play for them?

4. Spurs played Sheffield United in 1901, Manchester City in 1981 and Coventry City in 1987. All these clubs contained a player with the same surname, and in two of the three finals in question the man with that surname found the net. What was that surname?

5. Who scored the only goal of the game for Spurs against Wolves in the 1921 FA Cup Final?

6. Which Manchester City player scored at both ends in the 1-1 draw with Spurs in the 1981 FA Cup Final?

7. Which two Spurs players appeared in both the 1987 FA Cup Final against Coventry City and the 1991 FA Cup Final against Nottingham Forest?

8. Who is the only Spurs player to score in an FA Cup Final and an FA Cup Final replay in the same post-war season?

9. An unused substitute for Coventry City against Spurs in 1987 played for the London club in the 1991 final against Nottingham Forest. Who was he?

10. Whose own goal in the 1991 final against Forest decided the match in Spurs' favour?

QUIZ No. 14

FOOTBALLER OF THE YEAR

1. Who is the only Spurs player to win the 'Young Player of the Year' award twice?

2. Who was the only Spurs player to win the Football Writers' Association 'Player of the Year' award in the 1970s?

3. Which player won the Scottish PFA award in 1986 with Dundee United, joined Spurs and then went back to Scotland with Glasgow Rangers and won the Scottish Writers Award in his first season back in 1989?

4. Who is the only Spurs player to win the FWA award twice, in 1958 and 1961?

5. Typically, FIFA has now called the 'World Footballer of the Year' by three different titles. The last time I looked it was called the 'FIFA Best Player'. Anyway, no one has won it while at Spurs, but someone who has played for the club won it in 2018. Who was he?

6. The annual merit award has become something of a dog's breakfast, but which ex-Spurs player was a very deserving winner in 2000?

7. Who were the only two Spurs players to win the FWA award in the 1980s, one of them in 1982 and the other in 1987?

8. Who, in 1980, was the only player in the 20th century to win the 'Young Player of the Year' award while at Spurs?

9. Spurs players won the FWA award three times in the 1990s: in 1992, 1995 and 1999. Who were they?

10. Which Spurs player won the PFA award in 2011 and 2013?

FOREIGN IMPORTS - PART 1

Like most Premier League clubs, Spurs have played in the overseas market much more in this century than the previous one. You are given the purchase date and the player in each case. Which club did they come from?

1. Helder Postiga – 2003

2. Mido – 2005

3. Edgar Davids – 2005

4. Benoit Assou-Ekotto – 2006

5. Luka Modric – 2008

6. Jan Vertonghen – 2012

7. Lewis Holtby – 2013

8. Nacer Chadli – 2013

9. Juan Foyth – 2017

10. Lucas Moura – 2018

QUIZ No. 16

FOREIGN IMPORTS - PART 2

1. Y-P Lee – 2005

2. Dimitar Berbatov – 2006

3. Roman Pavlyuchenko – 2008

4. Rafa Van Der Vaart – 2010

5. Gylfi Sigurdsson – 2012

6. Christian Eriksen – 2013

7. Eric Dier – 2014

8. Toby Alderweireld – 2015

9. Kevin Nkoudou – 2016

10. Tanguy Ndombele – 2019

GOALKEEPERS - PART 1

1. Which Spurs goalkeeper holds a Premier League record in having played every game in eight successive seasons, although only the last one was with Spurs?

2. He played 44 games for Spurs between 1987 and 1990, but he ended up with two champions' medals, one with Everton before he joined Spurs and the other with Blackburn Rovers after he left. Who was he?

3. Around the turn of the century two goalkeepers whose names begin with the same letter played in goal for Spurs in the Premier League. One had just one appearance but the other played 64 times. They had both been at Wimbledon together five years before. Who were they?

4. Which post-war international goalkeeper for Spurs started out as a boxer?

5. Which Spurs and England goalkeeper, after he joined another Premier League club, had the rare experience of having his name on the front and back of his jersey?

6. Who is the only post-war goalkeeper to be capped with both Leeds United and Spurs?

7. Which two goalkeepers who have both played in post-war FA Cup finals against Spurs have also scored league goals?

8. Which two post-war Spurs goalkeepers, one playing over 200 league games while the other played just once, share the same surname?

9. Who is the only post-war Spurs goalkeeper to have two 'A's in a row in his surname?

10. Which two men, who played in goal for Chelsea in post-war FA Cup finals, later joined Spurs?

QUIZ No. 18

GOALKEEPERS - PART 2

1. Someone had to be unlucky enough to be in goal when Spurs lost 5-0 at home to Arsenal on 23 December 1978. Who was it? Sorry to bring that up by the way!

2. Who was the last goalkeeper to gain an FA Cup winner's medal playing for Spurs?

3. In what way could it be said that Pat Jennings and Heurelho Gomes had opposite experiences?

4. Who is the only Spurs goalkeeper with a World Cup winner's medal?

5. He only played in 25 league games for Spurs, but his seven FA Cup appearances were considerably more significant as they coincided with Spurs winning the trophy in 1981. Who was he?

6. He played 73 times in all competitions for Spurs between 1958 and 1964 and was somewhat unfortunate not to play a few more before he moved on to Southampton. If something goes wrong when you're baking a loaf you sometimes get this phenomenon. Who was he?

7. Six years before the answer to the previous question left for Southampton, another Spurs goalkeeper had made the same move, after playing 95 times in all competitions for the club. Who was he?

8. Which 21st-century Spurs goalkeeper began his career in England with another London club and, after Spurs, ended it with another London club?

9. This goalkeeper's career took in over 450 games between 1958 and 1972, mostly for Port Vale, Ipswich Town and Bury. Towards the end of it he played just three league games for Spurs or, as seems appropriate, nine half hours. Who was he?

10. These two goalkeepers together played over 500 games for Spurs in all competitions. One left the club in 1981, the year that the other one joined. When you say their names together, they sound like a well-known church and landmark in the Strand. Who are they?

QUIZ No. 19

HOTSPUR HIDINGS

These are the days that all supporters would prefer to forget, but they somehow linger in the memory as much as the good days.

1. In beating Spurs 7-2 on 1 September 1951, and by 7-1 on 28 December 1996, this northern club became the only one to score seven goals twice in a post-war league game against them. Who are they?

2. Which club, in 2013/2014, beat Spurs 6-0 and 5-1 in the two Premier League games they met in?

3. Although it wasn't official because it happened in wartime football, which Midlands club beat Spurs 8-0 in the last Football League South season on 6 October 1945?

4. I remember Butch Cassidy saying something of the sort to the Sundance Kid and, sure enough, time caught up with that great 'double' side, and although they could still hammer teams on occasion, they were increasingly vulnerable. Evidence for this came in season 1963/64 when they twice visited Lancashire and came home beaten 7-2 both times by teams beginning with the same letter. Who were the two teams?

5. Spurs have conceded eight goals in a league fixture just once. It happened in the season they were relegated, and came on 16 October 1976, when which Midlands club beat them 8-2?

6. On 31 October 1914, Spurs were beaten 7-2 away from home. One of Tottenham's scorers was called Bliss, but I imagine it was anything but! 64 years later on 2 September 1978 they shipped another seven on the same ground, only this time they failed to reply. Who beat them?

7. Spurs' biggest League Cup defeat happened on 27 November 1996 in Lancashire, when they went down 6-1 to which club?

8. That same score, 6-1, also constitutes their heaviest defeat in the FA Cup and has happened twice, once in Yorkshire in the sixth round of the 1927/28 season, and then again in the North East in a third-round replay in 1999/2000. Who were their conquerors?

9. Back in the mists of time, 1885 to be precise, on 7 November, Spurs lost 8-0 at home in the London Association Cup to a team that certainly didn't play as their name suggested they might! Who were they?

10. Which side with educational connections beat Spurs 8-2 on their own ground in the London Senior Cup on 13 October 1888?

QUIZ No. 20

INTERNATIONALS - ENGLAND

1. Which centre-forward, capped while with Spurs this century, has to do this in a heading duel with his opposing centre-half to make it a fair contest?

2. Which midfielder who played for England four times while with Spurs in 1987 had previously been in the England team that was knocked out of the World Cup by Maradona's cheating and brilliance combined?

3. If you want to know how many caps this 1970s Tottenham player earned while at the club and also what his name is, all you have to do is answer the following question: how many applications are recommended when painting a door?

4. When England were beaten 6-3 by Hungary at Wembley in 1953, which Spurs player scored one of the home side's goals from the penalty spot?

5. Did Paul Robinson win more England caps while at Spurs than the combined totals of Ted Ditchburn, Ray Clemence and Ian Walker at the club? Yes or no?

6. Which post-war striker had exactly one England goal for every two games played while at Spurs, finding the net 19 times in 38 outings?

7. Who is the only flower to be capped by England since the war while with Spurs?

8. Who are the only two players with names beginning with 'L' to have been capped by England while at Spurs this century?

9. Which is the only surname that has appeared twice since the war in Spurs players capped by England?

10. Who are the only three players with names starting with 'D' to be capped by England while with Spurs since the war?

QUIZ No. 21

INTERNATIONALS – SCOTLAND, WALES, NORTHERN IRELAND AND THE REPUBLIC OF IRELAND

1. When he played in the middle of the park for Spurs in the late 1950s and 1960s, he received 18 caps from the Scottish selectors who didn't much care for Anglo-Scots at the time. If they had given him 118 caps it still wouldn't have been enough. Who was he?

2. Which Spurs player is the only one to have captained his country at a World Cup tournament, and which country did he captain?

3. Which Spurs player made his debut for Wales against the Ukraine on 28 March 2001?

4. Which Spurs player scored the goal for Northern Ireland that knocked Spain out of the World Cup on their own soil in the group stage in 1982?

5. Full-back Chris Hughton won 50 Republic of Ireland caps between 1979 and 1990 while at Spurs. With which club did he win his final three?

6. Which two post-war Spurs goalkeepers have been capped for Scotland the same number of times?

7. Which Spurs central defender played for Scotland 33 times between 1995 and 1998?

8. He is the only Spurs player relevant to this section to have a surname beginning with a 'Y', and his eight caps came in 1979 and 1980. Who is he, and which country did he play for?

9. He shares his name with a well-known water biscuit and received his 18 Republic of Ireland caps while at Tottenham between 1999 and 2004. Who is he?

10. Who are the only two Welsh players to get to double figures in goals for Wales while at Spurs?

QUIZ No. 22

INTERNATIONALS - OVERSEAS - PART 1

Which countries did the following Spurs players represent?

1. Sergei Rebrov

2. Moussa Saib

3. Christian Eriksen

4. Heung-Min Son

5. Serge Aurier

6. Dimitar Berbatov

7. Erik Lamela

8. Ronny Rosenthal

9. Michel Vorm

10. Nico Claesen

QUIZ No. 23

INTERNATIONALS - OVERSEAS - PART 2

Which countries did the following Spurs players represent?

1. Davinson Sanchez

2. Moussa Sissoko

3. Ilie Dumitrescu

4. Steffen Iversen

5. Gudni Bergsson

6. Ramon Vega

7. Fernando Llorente

8. John Chiedozie

9. Victor Wanyama

10. Emmanuel Adebayor

QUIZ No. 24

JOBS FOR THE BOYS!

The following Spurs players all have names that are occupations. Can you identify them from the information given?

1. Member of the famous double-winning team who needs an early start in this job.

2. Came from Hull City in 1934 and left for Bolton Wanderers a year later, he shares his first name with a League Cup-winning Spurs manager, and his surname refers to someone who works with the world's most sought-after metal.

3. Tottenham central defender who joined the club in 1998. His job is a solitary one with a lot of power and high remuneration.

4. Another member of the double team who sounds like a policeman working in a forge.

5. Full-back signed from Wimbledon; his job involves climbing up ladders to work on roofs.

6. He didn't stay long at White Hart Lane, but he ended up with an FA Cup winner's medal by keeping goal for Spurs in the 1921 FA Cup Final. His job involves considerable patience, a strong constitution, and accuracy with a weapon.

7. Part of the Spurs team that won the UEFA Cup in 1984, he appears in Chaucer's *Canterbury Tales* and in 'A whiter shade of pale' by Procol Harum.

8. Stoneworker from Spurs' midfield this century, he might have been useful in helping to build the new ground.

9. Played 55 times for Spurs between 1936 and 1939, he shares a first name with the elder of the 'Steptoes', and his surname is someone who carries messages in hotels and can also be found in a book.

10. Defender who joined the club in 2000 from Port Vale, he almost shares his first name with someone who had a bit of a fling with a certain Egyptian woman, while we really need to stick an 'E' in the middle of his surname, but these things ceased to matter in progressive educational circles about 50 years ago. A fair bit of nurturing is involved here.

LEAGUE CUP FINALS

1. Who are the only club that Spurs have met in more than one League Cup Final?

2. Who are the only club that Spurs have met in a League Cup Final where the game has been decided by penalties?

3. Who scored Spurs' winning goal in the 1973 League Cup Final against Norwich City?

4. Who is the only player to score twice against Spurs in a League Cup Final?

5. Who got the winning goal for Spurs against Leicester City in the 1999 League Cup Final and which goalkeeper who conceded it later joined Spurs?

6. Who are the only club Spurs have met in a League Cup Final that were from a lower division?

7. Who is the only man to score twice in a League Cup Final for Spurs?

8. Spurs were involved in the first League Cup Final to be played under a sliding roof at the Millennium Stadium in Cardiff in 2002. They lost the game 2-1 to which club?

9. Who scored the Spurs goal in that final?

10. Who got the extra-time winner against Chelsea in the 2008 League Cup Final?

QUIZ No. 26

LONDON LINKS

There have been eight post-war England internationals who have been capped while at Spurs and other London clubs. You are given the dates of their complete England careers, their caps total and their position. Who are they in each case and with what other London club have they been capped?

1. 1966–74 – 67 caps – Midfield

2. 1993–98 – 17 caps – Centre-forward

3. 2014–17 – 13 caps – Forward

4. 1959–67 – 57 caps – Forward

5. 1996–2008 – 73 caps – Centre-half

6. 2004–13 – 18 caps – Midfield

7. 2001–16 – 34 caps – Midfield

8. 2006–12 – 13 caps – Centre-forward

9. Which London club is represented the most times besides Spurs?

10. Which player on the list is the only one to be capped while at four London clubs?

QUIZ No. 27

MAD MATCHES

1. Having lost there 6-0 the previous season, by what extremely rare score did Spurs lose by at Middlesbrough on 13 February 1915?

2. Which Midlands club did Spurs beat 7-4 in a league game at White Hart Lane on 27 March 1965?

3. The following March fans were treated to a high-scoring draw against another Midlands club, Aston Villa. So, if you've given Aston Villa as the answer to the previous question, you can discard them and have another go! What was the score?

4. Gary Lineker hit four goals on 21 September 1991, when Spurs beat Wimbledon in a league game at Plough Lane. What was the score?

5. On 19 September 1925, Spurs drew 5-5 at White Hart Lane with the side that had won the league in the previous two years, and would go on to win that year's as well. Who were they?

6. Spurs were drawn away to Leicester City on 10 January 1914, in the FA Cup third round. With what score line did they take them back to White Hart Lane for a replay that Spurs won 2-0?

7. On 29 December 2007, Spurs and Reading produced ten goals between them in a Premier League game at White Hart Lane. What was the score?

8. Fans who came to the last home game of the season at Wembley in May 2018 were treated to nine goals. Who were Spurs playing and what was the score?

9. Which Yorkshire club was beaten 7-3 by Spurs at White Hart Lane on 30 August 1926?

10. In December 1960, Spurs drew 4-4 at home with a Lancastrian club. In the same month two years later, they drew 4-4 at home again, this time with a London club who share the same colours as the earlier visitors. Who were their two opponents?

QUIZ No. 28

MANAGERS - PART 1

1. Who was the only man to win the League with Spurs as a player and a manager?

2. Which three post-war Spurs managers have all managed Southampton?

3. Who was the only Spurs manager to win the World Cup as a player?

4. Who was the only Spurs manager to captain another club to the Premier League title?

5. Besides Bill Nicholson, who is the only Spurs manager to lead them to a European trophy?

6. Whose first game managing Spurs coincided with the highest number of goals in a North London derby?

7. Which three Spurs managers have each had two spells of management at the club?

8. Who was the most recent Spurs manager to win a trophy at the club?

9. Which man who managed the club from 1997 to 1998 was keen to show everyone he had come to the ground by tube by showing his ticket?

10. Which Spurs manager won 12 England caps as a player with another London club?

MANAGERS – PART 2

1. Who is the only manager to have come to Spurs having won the Champions League previously in his managerial career?

2. Which three post-war Spurs managers all played for Arsenal?

3. Which canny Scot took over the managerial role at Tottenham while still a player at the club and led them to their first FA Cup success in 1901?

4. Which Spurs manager was sacked after a 5-0 defeat by Liverpool?

5. Who was manager of the 'push and run' side that won the title in 1950/51?

6. Spurs manager between 1935 and 1938, he had played for West Ham United against Bolton Wanderers in the legendary first Wembley FA Cup Final of 1923. Who was he?

7. Whose reign as Spurs manager lasted just a few months between June and November of 2004?

8. Spurs manager between 1907 and 1908, Fred Kirkham had been previously involved in the 1906 FA Cup Final between Everton and Newcastle United. What role did he play?

9. Doug Livermore, Spurs head coach from 1992 to 1993, played over 100 games for which club between 1970 and 1974?

10. Who resigned his position as Spurs manager to allow Bill Nicholson to take over in October 1958?

QUIZ No. 30

MULTIPLE CHOICE

1. Since 1966, the media and sponsors have chosen their 'Manager of the Year'. Who is the only Spurs manager to win it?
(a) Bill Nicholson (b) Keith Burkinshaw (c) Harry Redknapp (d) Mauricio Pochettino

2. Three surnames that appeared in the Spurs team that won the FA Cup in 1901 reappeared in the team that won it in 1961. Whose is the only name here that didn't feature in both finals?
(a) Brown (b) Jones (c) Smith (d) White

3. Spurs have experienced relegation from the top flight on four occasions, and five clubs have accompanied them on the way down. These are Middlesbrough, Leicester City, Stoke City, Sunderland and one London club. Which one?
(a) Chelsea (b) Crystal Palace (c) Fulham (d) Charlton

4. Spurs have finished runners-up in the top flight five times. The four clubs below all finished above them to win the league, but which one has done that twice?
(a) Everton (b) Chelsea (c) Liverpool (d) Manchester United

5. Which goalkeeper has not played in goal for Spurs in a European final?
(a) Bill Brown (b) Ray Clemence (c) Pat Jennings (d) Tony Parks

6. Former players Alan Mullery, Peter Taylor, Chris Hughton and Gus Poyet have all managed which club?
(a) Birmingham City (b) Brentford (c) Bournemouth (d) Brighton

7. Which Spurs player made exactly 300 league appearances for the club?
(a) Mike England (b) Alan Mullery (c) Bill Nicholson (d) Peter Baker

8. When Spurs beat Atletico Madrid 5-1 to win the European Cup Winners' Cup in 1963, who scored the Spaniards' goal?
(a) Collar (b) Tie (c) Shirt (d) Jacket

9. Which Spurs player was not substituted in the Champions League
    Final against Liverpool in Madrid on 1 June 2019?
    (a) Harry Winks (b) Moussa Sissoko (c) Dele Alli (d) Harry Kane

10. Spurs scored 20 goals on their run to that Champions League Final,
    but who scored their opener in a 2-1 defeat at Inter Milan in their
    first group match on 18 September 2018?
    (a) Christian Eriksen (b) Heung-Min Son (c) Lucas Moura
    (d) Erik Lamela

QUIZ No. 31

NOT SO HOT SPURS! (GIANT KILLING)

1. Which non-league club knocked Spurs out of the FA Cup 3-2 in the third round of 1909/10 after Spurs had themselves accounted for Plymouth Argyle and Chelsea?

2. Three years later it happened again when, after beating Blackpool after a replay, Spurs succumbed to a side geographically close to the one that had beaten them in 1910. Who beat them?

3. In the last season before World War One Spurs finished bottom of the First Division and so they were rather vulnerable to an FA Cup upset. They did well to beat Sunderland, but then lost to which non-league side in the east of the country?

4. A goal from Neil Ruddock was not enough to save Spurs losing 2-1 to which Third Division club in the FA Cup fourth round of 1987/88?

5. Spurs were extremely susceptible to being turned over in the FA Cup in the 1950s. In fact, it happened at two-yearly intervals in 1955, 1957 and 1959. In the first of them they went down 3-1 away in the fifth round after a long trip north on an icy pitch. You can view the Division Three North side beating them on the internet if it doesn't hurt too much. Who were they?

6. 1957 brought a defeat by the same score line in the same round, but this time by a Division Three South club who had already knocked out Wolves at Molineux in the previous round. Who were they?

7. The 1960s brought much better things in the FA Cup, but there was one more humiliation to endure before the 1950s were out. It came yet again in the fifth round to a Division Three South team who beat Spurs 1-0 in a replay after a late Cliff Jones goal had saved them in the first game at White Hart Lane. Who beat them? If you've got question three right, why change your answer?

8. In 1976/77 Spurs were knocked out of the League Cup by a Third Division side 3-2 at White Hart Lane. Who beat them?

9. Spurs suffered a similar fate in the League Cup again in 1978/79 when, at the first hurdle, after a 2-2 away draw they lost 3-1 at home to a side from the Third Division who play in the same colours as Spurs. Who were they?

10. Who were the only club from the fourth flight of English football to knock Spurs out of the League Cup this century until another club, covered elsewhere, repeated the trick in 2019/20?

QUIZ No. 32

ODD MAN OUT

Who is the odd man out in each group of five Spurs players?

1. Jermaine Jenas, Stephen Carr, Moussa Sissoko, Paul Gascoigne, Les Ferdinand

2. Jamie Clapham, John Scales, Jason Cundy, Steve Sedgley, Alan Brazil

3. Terry Medwin, Tom Carroll, Michel Vorm, Ben Davies, Fernando Llorente

4. Darren Anderton, Nico Kranjcar, Paul Walsh, Peter Crouch, Younes Kaboul

5. Mark Bowen, Ian Culverhouse, Ian Crook, Maurice Norman, Jimmy Neighbour

6. David Howells, Gareth Bale, Alf Ramsey, Victor Wanyama, Martin Chivers

7. Freddie Kanoute, Paul Allen, Michael Carrick, Jermaine Defoe, Martin Peters

8. Willie Young, Sol Campbell, Laurie Brown, Freddie Cox, Jimmy Robertson

9. Gerry Armstrong, Arthur Grimsdell, Mark Falco, Tommy Harmer, Heurelho Gomes

10. Jamie Redknapp, Christian Ziege, Oyvind Leonhardsen, Paul Stewart, Ronny Rosenthal

ONE-CAP WONDERS

Can you identify these players who were all capped once for England while at Spurs?

1. Full-back whose sole cap came against Scotland in 1954.

2. Spurs midfielder who received his only England cap as a substitute in a 1-1 draw with Italy in Turin on 31 March 2015.

3. Full-back whose only cap came in a 5-2 defeat by France in Alf Ramsey's first game as England's manager on 27 February 1963.

4. Midfielder whose cap came against Iceland on 2 June 1982.

5. Left-winger whose only England appearance came in the legendary match at Wembley on 25 November 1953, when Hungary beat us 6-3.

6. Defender who came on as a substitute against Israel on 11 February 1988.

7. Defender whose only international moment came on 3 October 1951, against France.

8. Midfielder who managed to score with his first kick in international football when England played Portugal in 1951, but was never selected again, giving him the best strike rate of any post-war Spurs player.

9. Defender whose solitary game in an England shirt came against Sweden in 2004.

10. Defender whose one cap unfortunately came in 2012 on the night that Sweden's Ibrahimovic took England apart and helped himself to four goals.

QUIZ No. 34

THE 100 CLUB

The number changes as time passes, but at the time of writing I believe 17 players have scored 100 or more goals for Spurs in all competitions. My apologies to those whose achievement went unmentioned.

1. Who, on 27 September 1919, in a 6-1 win over Lincoln City, became the first man to reach 100 goals for Spurs, going on to record 105 before managing the club as well?

2. Which two men with surnames starting with a 'K' are members of the 100 club?

3. The top man, on 268 goals, scored exactly twice as many as someone who played up front with him and is the only Scot on the list. Who are the two players?

4. Who is the only player on the list to score his goals in two different centuries?

5. Martin Chivers managed 181 goals, an impressive record, and an unusual aspect here was that his first and last goals for Spurs came against teams from the same city. Which city?

6. Only two players have got through the 200 barrier. Who was the first to do so before leaving Spurs in 1964?

7. Two players were regular goalscorers between the end of the war and the mid-1950s, scoring 249 between them. Who were they?

8. One of the players in the '100 club' scored 138 times for Spurs between 1930 and 1937 before being the only one to also play for Arsenal. Who was he?

9. Who is the only member of the '100 club' to score the winning goal in a Tyne-Wear Derby? And what a brilliant goal it was!

10. Who is the only player that could be described as a midfielder to reach 100 goals for Spurs?

QUIZ No. 35

SCOTTISH SPURS

Back in the day, Scots played a big part in English football. Which Scottish clubs did these well-known Spurs players come from? Clubs can appear more than once in this section.

1. Steve Archibald – 1980

2. Bill Brown – 1959

3. Alfie Conn – 1974

4. John Duncan – 1974

5. Alan Gilzean – 1964

6. Alan Hutton – 2008

7. Dave Mackay – 1959

8. Neil McNab – 1973

9. Jimmy Robertson – 1963

10. John White – 1959

SPURS V ARSENAL - ASSORTMENT

1. He only played 28 times for Spurs before joining Barcelona, but has a place in the memories of Spurs fans for welcoming in the new year on 2 January 1995 with a winning goal in the Premier League at White Hart Lane. Who was he?

2. What a game to make your debut in! Which member of the double-winning side played his first game for the club in a pulsating 4-4 draw between the clubs at Highbury on 22 February 1958?

3. The 1990s produced the only season when both league matches between the clubs ended 0-0. What season was it?

4. The league game at Highbury in the 1992/93 season was played on 11 May 1993, a few days before Arsenal were due to play Sheffield Wednesday in the FA Cup Final. George Graham, Arsenal's manager, put out a seriously weakened side and Spurs took full advantage in winning 3-1. I knew someone who didn't renew his season ticket because Graham had failed to realise what the season's most important fixture was! Teddy Sheringham scored one of the goals which would have pleased him no end, but who got the other two, turning out to be the only Spurs player in that decade to score twice against the old enemy in a league game?

5. Spurs and Arsenal have played numerous 'friendlies' against each other over the years. On 29 April 1912, they met each other at Park Royal to raise money for what?

6. The first record of a meeting between the clubs was a friendly on 19 November 1887. No one knows the teams or scores, but Spurs led 2-1 on 75 minutes when what brought the game to a halt?

7. What was special about Jimmy Robertson's goal for Spurs in a 3-1 home win over Arsenal on 10 October 1964?

8. In the 1963/64 season someone did something unique in the Spurs v Arsenal story by playing for each team against the other in the same season. Who was he?

9. The first time that a player from both sides was sent off in a Spurs v Arsenal encounter came on 29 March 1982 at White Hart Lane in a 2-2 draw. Alan Sunderland was in the 'red corner', who was in the 'blue corner'?

10. Roy Low only appeared on a football pitch eight times for Spurs. Why did his name enter the annals of the North London Derby on 11 September 1965 in a 2-2 draw at White Hart Lane?

QUIZ No. 37

SPURS V ARSENAL - THE FA CUP

1. In which decade did Spurs and Arsenal meet each other for the first time in the FA Cup?

2. How many times have they been drawn against each other in the FA Cup?

3. Have they ever drawn an FA Cup tie against each other?

4. Spurs had their first FA Cup victory over Arsenal on 2 January 1982 at White Hart Lane. Who scored the only goal of the game?

5. What is the only league ground on which Spurs have played Arsenal in an FA Cup semi-final?

6. The 1991 semi-final win over Arsenal lives long in the memory of Spurs fans, certainly longer than the one two years later! Which two Spurs players scored in their 3-1 win at Wembley?

7. Who scored Spurs' goal when they lost 2-1 to Arsenal in the FA Cup semi-final of 2001?

8. Which Spurs manager was sacked just before that semi-final?

9. Whichever team has prevailed when Spurs have met Arsenal in the FA Cup has always reached that year's final. True or false?

10. The attendance record for an FA Cup tie between Spurs and Arsenal is 77,893. In which year was it set?

QUIZ No. 38

SPURS V ARSENAL –
THE LEAGUE 1909-99

1. With 98 Spurs goals he just failed to qualify for the '100 club', but he was popular with Spurs fans in the 1927/28 season when scoring in both matches against Arsenal, getting two in a 3-1 home win and Spurs' goal in a 1-1 draw away from home. Who was he?

2. In this whole period only one Spurs player has scored a hat-trick in a league game against Arsenal. It came on 26 August 1961 at White Hart Lane in a 4-3 Spurs win. Who got it?

3. Who is the only post-war Spurs player with a surname beginning with an 'F' to score against Arsenal in a league game?

4. Two players who share a surname but are not related have scored for Spurs against Arsenal in the post-war period, the earlier one scored several times in the 1960s, while the more recent scored just once in the 1980s. Who are the two players?

5. Two more players who share a surname, but this time are related, have scored for Spurs against Arsenal in the post-war period. The first did so in the 1960s and the second did so in the 1980s. Who were they?

6. Which three Spurs players with a 'Z' in their surname have scored for Spurs against Arsenal in the league?

7. Who scored for Spurs against Arsenal in a 2-2 draw at White Hart Lane on 27 December 1976, and then crossed North London to become an Arsenal player?

8. Spurs' biggest league win against Arsenal came at White Hart Lane on Christmas Day of 1911. They matched the score-line on the same ground on 4 April 1983. What was that score?

9. Who, on 16 April 1910, in a 1-1 draw at White Hart Lane, scored Tottenham's first Football League goal against Arsenal who, at the time, were known as Woolwich Arsenal because they hadn't yet decamped north of the river?

10. Which Spurs player, with ten to his name, holds the record for the most league goals for Spurs against Arsenal in the period covered here?

QUIZ No. 39

SPURS V ARSENAL – THE LEAGUE 2000-20

1. Who has been, on 6 November 2016, in a 1-1 draw at the Emirates, the only Spurs player to score an own goal against Arsenal in this 20-year period?

2. Starting with the last two goals of the 4-5 defeat against Arsenal at White Hart Lane on 13 November 2004, there was a run of five Spurs goals in the Derby over the next two years that all came from players whose names began with the same letter. Who were the three players?

3. In 2010/11 Spurs drew 3-3 at home and won 3-2 at the Emirates. Who scored from the penalty spot for them in both games?

4. How many players scored for Spurs against Arsenal in the two league games played at Wembley in 2017/18 and 2018/19?

5. In this period only one Spurs player with a surname starting with a 'C' has scored in the league against Arsenal. It happened on 27 September 2014 in a 1-1 draw at the Emirates. Who was that player?

6. Who scored Tottenham's first league goal at the Emirates Stadium when Spurs went down 2-1 in season 2007/08?

7. Which four players with surnames beginning with the first letter of the alphabet have scored for Spurs against Arsenal between 2000 and 2020?

8. Everyone knows about the famous fightback that concluded with a 4-4 draw away to Arsenal on the night of 29 October 2008. All eight goals were scored by different players. Three of these eight players ended their careers having played for both Spurs and Arsenal. Which three?

9. A tough one! Who are the only two players to have scored away to Arsenal in the Premier League that have also scored a goal in an FA Cup Final?

10. Who are the only two players to score twice in a match for Spurs against Arsenal in this period?

QUIZ No. 40

SPURS V ARSENAL - THE LEAGUE CUP

1. In the FA Cup it took 55 years for Spurs and Arsenal to come out of the hat together, but in the League Cup they clashed before the new tournament was a decade old, in season 1967/68. Arsenal won the two-leg affair 2-1 on aggregate. Who was on the mark for Spurs?

2. Spurs finally got their revenge for that defeat when beating Arsenal 1-0 in the fourth round on 4 November 1980 at White Hart Lane. Whose goal did the trick?

3. It was Arsenal's turn again to have bragging rights in the competition when they went to White Hart Lane in the third round on 9 November 1983 and ran out 2-1 winners. Spurs' goal came from a penalty. Who took it?

4. When the teams played each other again in the competition in the 1986/87 season it proved to be a contest of epic proportions which Spurs somehow contrived to lose after three matches in which they were never behind in the overall situation until the last few minutes. Which Spurs player scored in each of the three games?

5. The clubs were joined in battle again in this competition in the new century when they met each other in the two-leg semi-final of 2006/07. Once again, Spurs frustrated their supporters by throwing away a great opportunity to reach the final. After leading 2-0 at half-time in the first game, they allowed Arsenal back in to draw 2-2, and then lost the second leg after extra time. Who opened the scoring for Spurs in the first match?

6. The fact that the second leg went to extra-time was down to a Spurs player equalising five minutes from time in the away leg. Who scored the goal?

7. These clubs couldn't get enough of each other in this competition, meeting again at the semi-final stage in 2007/08. This time it was the turn of Spurs. After a 1-1 away draw they took Arsenal apart at White Hart Lane, with Tim Sherwood pulling the strings from midfield, running out winners by 5-1 on the night and 6-2 on aggregate. Which Spurs player found the net in both games?

8. It was like they were magnets! 2010/11 brought yet another meeting when Spurs succumbed 4-1 in extra time at White Hart Lane after the 90 minutes of the third round had produced a 1-1 score-line on 21 September 2010. Who had scored for Spurs early in the second half?

9. The clubs met again in the same round in 2015/16, and the 2-1 defeat Spurs suffered on their own ground was disappointing. Not only did they lose, but an Arsenal player scored their goal. Who?

10. Spurs had the last laugh for the time being when they won 2-0 at the Emirates in the quarter-final of the 2018/19 season. Who scored their goals in an ill-tempered affair?

QUIZ No. 41

SPURS IN THE FA CUP 1894-1939

1. Which club, on 13 October 1894, were Tottenham's first opponents in an FA Cup tie?

2. It scarcely seems probable, but which club that shared their colours with Spurs did they meet in each of their first five seasons of FA Cup football?

3. From the following list of nine clubs, eight of them knocked Spurs out of the FA Cup pre-World War One, and in the inter-war years. One of the nine never played Spurs at all in the FA Cup in those years. Who is the odd one out: Aston Villa, Blackburn Rovers, Liverpool, Luton Town, Manchester City, Preston North End, Reading, Sheffield Wednesday or West Bromwich Albion?

4. When Spurs won the FA Cup as a Southern League club in 1901, one of their players created a record that still stands by scoring 15 FA Cup goals. Who was he?

5. In 1921, when they won the trophy again, they played a Lancastrian club in the semi-final at Hillsborough on their way to the final. They met the same club at the same stage of the competition on the same ground the following year, but this time their luck ran out. Who were the club?

6. Spurs were fortunate on two occasions in this period. On 20 February 1904, they were losing 1-0 at home to Aston Villa in front of 32,000 when the match was abandoned due to concerns about the crowd spilling on to the pitch. When it was played again, Spurs won 1-0 at Villa Park. Their second slice of good fortune had come earlier, on 2 November 1895, when Vampires drew blood by beating them 4-2. This match was declared void and Spurs beat them 2-1 when it was replayed. The very best of luck in answering this question which asks why it was replayed?

7. Spurs biggest FA Cup victory in this period came on 15 January 1923. Two days before, Worksop Town of the Midland League had put up a great display to hold Spurs 0-0 at White Hart Lane. They decided to cede ground advantage in the replay and paid the price. What was the score in the second match at White Hart Lane?

8. Spurs met the same West Country club in the third round of the FA Cup in the first two seasons back after World War One, beating them 3-1 away in 1919/20, and doubling that up to 6-2 at White Hart Lane in 1920/21, the first step on the road to winning the trophy. Who did they knock out at the same stage in successive seasons?

9. Spurs had two 7-1 home wins in the competition during these years, firstly against Devonian opposition in season 1909/10, and secondly in the last season before World War Two against a team a few miles north west of White Hart Lane. Which two teams did they beat?

10. In the final season before war brought an end to things, Spurs drew 3-3 and 1-1 with another London club in the fourth round of the competition, thereby necessitating a third match on a neutral ground. The ground chosen was naturally that of another London club, who would have had to disguise their pleasure when Spurs lost 2-1. Who did they play and what was the venue?

QUIZ No. 42

SPURS IN THE FA CUP 1946-60

1. Spurs reached three FA Cup semi-finals in this period but lost them all. A trial run for the current nightmare where they have done something unheard of in losing eight semi-finals in a row. They lost to Manchester City in 1956, and one club knocked them out twice, in 1948 and 1953. Who were they?

2. Spurs knocked out one club three times at White Hart Lane. They won 5-2 in 1948, 2-0 in 1957 and 4-0 in 1958. They also met this club in an FA Cup Final after this period. Who were they?

3 Which Welsh club that Spurs met again recently in the competition did they beat 4-1 at home and 4-0 away in successive seasons in 1959 and 1960?

4. Who, with a total of 17 goals, was Tottenham's leading FA Cup goalscorer of this period?

5. Spurs were taken to three matches just once in these years. It was in season 1952/53 in the sixth round when which Midlands club were beaten 1-0 at Molineux after 1-1 and 2-2 draws in the tie?

6. What did Freddie Cox, Tommy Harmer and Cliff Jones do in FA Cup ties in this period that no other Spurs player did?

7. Who were the only London club that Spurs knocked out twice in this space of time, firstly by 2-1 at White Hart Lane in a sixth-round replay in 1956, and then with a 2-0 third-round win at White Hart Lane in 1959?

8. Spurs biggest FA Cup win came on the night of 3 February 1960 at White Hart Lane. Their opponents, who went down 13-2, have been covered elsewhere, but which Spurs player scored five goals that night?

9. Two goalkeepers shared the 20 games Spurs played in the three seasons they reached the FA Cup semi-finals in 1948, 1953 and 1956. Who were they?

10. Who was the only Spurs player in this time frame to find the net in four successive FA Cup ties? It happened in the 1953/54 season.

QUIZ No. 43

SPURS IN CUP COMPETITIONS – THE 1960s

1. Spurs were knocked out of the FA Cup by the eventual winners just once during the decade. It happened in 1969 when which club beat them in the sixth round before going on to win the trophy?

2. Which London club knocked Spurs out of the FA Cup in successive years in 1964 and 1965?

3. Who scored a hat-trick for Spurs against Burnley in a 4-3 win in the FA Cup fourth round on 12 February 1966?

4. When Spurs lifted the FA Cup in 1961 to complete their famous 'double' only one club took them to a replay on the road to Wembley. It happened in the sixth round against a Second Division club who lost the White Hart Lane replay 5-0 after giving Spurs a real scare in a 1-1 draw in the first game. Who were they?

5. Who was the only Spurs player to score two hat-tricks in domestic cup competitions in this decade? They came against Torquay United in the FA Cup in 1965, and against Exeter City in the League Cup in 1968, both at White Hart Lane.

6. Mention of Torquay and Exeter leads us to Plymouth Argyle. I'm not certain, but I would be surprised if many clubs have been drawn against all three Devonian clubs in cup competitions in the same decade. But that's what happened to Spurs in the 1960s. They visited Argyle on 27 January 1962 for an FA Cup fourth-round tie. You know Spurs got through because they won the FA Cup that year, but by what score did they win the game?

7. Which club did Spurs meet four times in the FA Cup in the decade?

8. Spurs had somewhat grudgingly entered the League Cup in its seventh season of 1966/67 when they lost 1-0 away at the first hurdle to another London club. Which one?

9. Which Midlands club did Spurs defeat on four occasions in domestic cup competitions in the decade, three times in the FA Cup and once in the League Cup?

10. When Spurs were drawn away to Millwall in the FA Cup third round in January 1967 and made the short trip across London to The Den, they came away with a 0-0 draw and won the replay. However, legend has it that one Spurs player, after he ended up in the crowd, came back out again minus his shorts! Which Spurs player was it?

QUIZ NO. 44

SPURS IN CUP COMPETITIONS – THE 1970s

1. The 1970s were a terrible decade for Spurs in the FA Cup. Such a contrast to the 1960s when they won the trophy three times. In the ten seasons how many times did Spurs go out in the third round?

2. 1972 proved to be the only year that Spurs went out of the FA Cup at the hands of the eventual winners. Who were they?

3. Which team from the North East did Spurs play five matches against in the League Cup over the decade?

4. The League Cup proved to be a better proposition for Spurs in this decade. They won it in 1971 and 1973 and had good runs in other years as well. In that first win of 1971, which club did Spurs beat 4-2 on aggregate in the semi-final?

5. It's a long journey to this place, but Spurs won there 3-2 on 23 January 1971 in the FA Cup fourth round. The following season they drew them again, this time in the third round at home. But Spurs could only draw 1-1 and made the long trek north again on 18 January 1972. They came out winners by 3-1. Who were their opponents?

6. Which club provided unwanted bookends to the decade by knocking Spurs out of the FA Cup in 1970/71 and 1979/80?

7. When Spurs won the League Cup again in 1973, the club they beat in the semi-final must have produced some slight déjà-vu because Spurs had beaten them in a two-leg affair in another competition the previous year, winning away and drawing at home, just like this time. Who did they beat in the semi-final and which tournament had they met in the year before?

8. In 1978/79 and 1979/80 Spurs played the same club four times in a row in the FA Cup, losing to them after a replay in the sixth round of 1978/79 and beating them after a replay in the third round of the following season. Who were they?

9. Spurs met two non-league sides over the decade in the FA Cup. The first was a south-coast town who were beaten 6-0 in the third round of 1972/73, and the other was a side who came to White Hart Lane and earned a 1-1 draw before Spurs won the replay 3-0. Who were the two non-league teams and which ground was used for the replay?

10. Spurs scored seven goals just once in cup competitions during the decade, in the League Cup at White Hart Lane against Yorkshire opposition on 3 December 1975. Who were the visitors?

QUIZ No. 45

SPURS IN CUP COMPETITIONS – THE 1980s

1. Spurs left the 1970s behind in the FA Cup when the 1980s arrived, winning the trophy in 1981 and 1982. Which London club did they beat in the competition in both those years?

2. Over the decade 15 clubs knocked Spurs out of domestic cup competitions, but they included just one Yorkshire club who beat Spurs in the FA Cup third round of 1988/89. Who were they?

3. Spurs played in three FA Cup semi-finals in the decade and won them all. Happy Days! The years were 1981, 1982 and 1987. Who were the three beaten semi-finalists?

4. Although the League Cup adventure of 1986/87 ended badly with defeat to Arsenal in the semi-final, on the way Spurs scored five goals on three occasions. They beat a Yorkshire club 5-3, a Midlands club 5-0 and a London club 5-0, all at White Hart Lane. Who were the three beaten clubs?

5. Clive Allen was on fire in that 1986/87 season. He scored three times as many League Cup goals as he did FA Cup goals. What was his total over the two competitions?

6. Who got a hat-trick for Spurs at Halifax when they won a League Cup tie there 5-1 on 26 September 1984?

7. In 1981/82 Spurs reached the League Cup Final, going down 3-1 to Liverpool. In the semi-final they saw off West Bromwich Albion 1-0 on aggregate. Who got the decisive goal in the second leg at White Hart Lane?

8. Spurs met four London clubs in the League Cup of 1980/81, playing six matches in all without leaving London. Who were their four opponents and which one put paid to Spurs' chance of winning it?

9. Which Spurs midfielder was the only player to score for them in both domestic cup competitions in 1989/90? He scored at home to Southampton in the FA Cup, and at home to Tranmere Rovers in the League Cup.

10. Another Spurs midfielder, whose surname begins with the same letter as the answer to the previous question, got two goals in the 1987 FA Cup semi-final at Villa Park. Who was he?

QUIZ No. 46

SPURS IN CUP COMPETITIONS - 1990s

1. Who were the only club that met Spurs in more than one FA Cup semi-final during this decade?

2. During the 1990s three clubs who share Spurs' colours knocked them out of the League Cup. Who were they?

3. Who was the only Spurs player to register four goals in a cup game during this time? He did it in a 5-0 win over Hartlepool United at White Hart Lane in the League Cup on 26 September 1990.

4. In this decade Spurs twice scored six goals away from home. Both instances came in the 1994/95 season, the first in a 6-3 win in the League Cup, and the second in an FA Cup replay win by 6-2. Which two teams did they knock out?

5. On the night of 17 January 1996, Hereford United visited White Hart Lane for an FA Cup third-round replay and went down 5-1. Who scored a hat-trick for Spurs in that game, and what did Hereford bring with them to scare the home side?

6. Two non-league sides came to White Hart Lane in the FA Cup third round, the first in 1993 and the second in 1995, going down 5-1 and 3-0 respectively. In the first instance, the team who had taken part in the very first FA Cup season of 1871/72 had given up home advantage, while the other club had met Spurs on the same ground in the same competition 16 years before. Who were the two teams?

7. In the FA Cup, Spurs met the same team two years running in 1997/98 and 1998/99. On the first occasion Spurs were swept out of the competition by the underdogs in a fourth-round replay. The following year they gained revenge with a 1-0 away win in round six. Who were their opposition and whose stunning goal won the second match?

8. Spurs drew the same London club at the first League Cup hurdle in 1992/93 and 1998/99, beating them in all four games by 4-2, 3-1 and 3-2 twice. Who were they?

9. Spurs met the same club in the last FA Cup tie they played in the 1998/99 season that they played in their first tie of the following season. Which club?

10. London, in the shape of Chelsea and Fulham, was a city from which two teams knocked Spurs out of the League Cup in the course of the decade. Which other city's two teams also managed that feat?

QUIZ No. 47

SPURS IN THE FOOTBALL LEAGUE
- 1908-39

1. In their first season of league football in the Second Division in 1908/09, Spurs were promoted by finishing runners-up to which northern club?

2. Spurs won their first Football League fixture at White Hart Lane on 1 September 1908, by 3-0. Who were the visitors from the Midlands?

3. What was unique in Spurs' history about the 0-0 home draw with Bradford City on 29 January 1910? Steel yourself for the answer!

4. What did Billy Minter do in a 4-0 win over Blackburn Rovers on 28 March 1910?

5. Spurs made an appalling start to the 1912/13 season, when it took them until 23 November before they recorded their first win in their 13th game. Lucky for some! The following season saw a much better opening when they won the first three games. However, at the end of it they occupied exactly the same lowly position as the previous one. What position?

6. In 1914/15, the final season before the war, Spurs were relegated, but bounced back in the first season after the conflict in 1919/20 when 31 of their 102 goals were scored by which player?

7. For some reason best known to themselves, the authorities of the time persisted with playing matches in blocks of two, home and away, against the same club. It did, however, enable Spurs to thrash another London club 5-0 at home and 4-0 away within the space of a week in October 1920. Who were their victims?

8. In 1921/22 Spurs attained their highest league position to that point when they finished second. However, the following year they dropped to 12th, and 15th in the one after. In that 1923/24 season a Spurs player scored his first goal for the club against Newcastle United on 19 January 1924. He went on to play 158 games for the club and became, after his playing career finished, the trainer of the Spurs side that won the League and FA Cup in 1960/61. Who was he?

9. 1927/28 was the strangest season thus far. With eight games left, Spurs were comfortably mid-table with 14 wins balanced by 14 defeats. After the eight games were played, they were relegated one point adrift of seven clubs. With just 16 more points they would have won the league! As it was, four goals from 'Taffy' O'Callaghan at the home of the eventual champions gave Spurs a 5-3 away win on 11 February 1928. Who were the eventual champions?

10. Spurs spent five years in Division Two before coming up again as runners-up in 1932/33, but stayed just two years in the top flight before another relegation. Which club came up with them in 1932/33?

QUIZ No. 48

SPURS IN THE FOOTBALL LEAGUE 1946-60

1. Spurs spent the first three seasons after the war in sixth, eighth and fifth place in Division Two. Perhaps it was a good omen that in the final day of the 1948/49 season they won 5-0 away at Plymouth Argyle. Their leading goalscorer for that season rounded things off with a hat-trick. Who was he?

2. The two Sheffield clubs and Southampton had to be separated by goal average for second place but in 1949/50 Spurs were away over the hill, winning the league by nine points. Their biggest win of the season came on 12 November at White Hart Lane by 7-0. It was against one of the three clubs mentioned above. Which one?

3. Spurs took the First Division by surprise in 1950/51, storming to the title and gaining just one point less than they did in their promotion season the year before. Only two clubs before Spurs had won the league in their first season up after promotion, and only two more have done it since. Who are the four clubs?

4. Which team did Spurs beat 6-1 at home in 1950/51 and 6-1 away the following season?

5. In that 1951/52 season Spurs finished second to Manchester United. They were helped on their way by a strange incident at White Hart Lane on 2 April 1952 as their game reached the closing stages. An Eddie Baily corner struck the referee in the back and rebounded to Baily, whose cross was headed in by Len Duquemin for a winning goal that shouldn't have stood. Which later relegated club were Spurs playing and which club, don't laugh, did Spurs edge out of second place in the league because of it being given?

6. From this point on Spurs became extremely unpredictable to say the least. The defence became a major headache. Surely no side before or since could, in five successive seasons, start out conceding 35 and then go to 44, then 51, then 69, and finally 76. Death by rising increments! This contributed to them finishing 16th twice and 18th and looking, as 1956/57 began, that they were finally going through the trap door. Where did they finish that season?

7. They racked up 104 goals in that season of 1956/57, which might make you want to adjust your answer to the previous question! Strangely enough, with all those goals, nobody reached 20 league goals. But how many players reached double figures?

8. In 1957/58 they came third, but again the defence wasn't great, conceding 14 more than Leeds United who came 17th. On 18 September 1957, they entertained Birmingham City at White Hart Lane. It was probably a bit more entertainment than their visitors were looking for as Spurs won 7-1, with which player scoring five times?

9. As most Spurs fans know, they beat Everton 10-4 on 11 October 1958 and this match has been covered elsewhere, but of which Spurs player in that game was it said in one Sunday newspaper the next day that 'he scored one and made the other nine'?

10. In that 1958/59 season Spurs finished 18th, coming close to relegation again, despite scoring more goals than Bolton Wanderers who came fourth. But in 1959/60 they suddenly started playing a brand of football that on its day put the rest of the league in the shade. A lot of good it did them in the end, because they lost two vital home games 1-0 at Easter to Manchester City and Chelsea. However, brushing that disappointment aside, they went away to turn in a magnificent display when their 3-1 win stopped which club winning three successive titles, and, more importantly, stopped them being the first side of the century to perform the coveted league and cup double? And we all know what happened next!

QUIZ No. 49

SPURS IN THE FOOTBALL LEAGUE – THE 1960s

1. Having given enough attention to the 1960/61 season elsewhere, we'll start with 1961/62. Which new kids on the block, although 'kids' is the wrong word in their case, were the only team to do the league double over Spurs in this season, on their way to winning the title for the only time in their history?

2. Spurs stayed comfortably in the top half of the table until the last season of the decade when they finished exactly halfway, but there was a falling away of goals scored. In 1962/63, when they finished second, they scored 111 goals, 27 more than champions Everton. In 1969/70 did they score 27, 37, 47 or 57 fewer goals than in 1962/63?

3. On which London ground did Spurs win 6-1 on 25 August 1962?

4. Over the Easter period of 1963, Spurs were beaten 5-2 on Good Friday, but put that right with a vengeance on Easter Monday by hammering the same opponents 7-2 at White Hart Lane with Jimmy Greaves claiming four of them. Who were their opponents?

5. In 1963/64 Spurs continued their Jekyll and Hyde stuff, shown clearly when they lost 7-2 away on 7 September 1963 and then won 6-1 the following Saturday at White Hart Lane. The two clubs involved shared the first five letters of their names. Who were they?

6. Which Spurs player got a league hat-trick three seasons running in seasons 1963/64, 1964/65 and 1965/66?

7. In 1966/67 Spurs finished third and won the FA Cup, but with a better start they could have had another 'double' on their hands. They went six games without a win in October and November, but how many of their last 20 league games did they lose?

8. An oddball question! During that 1966/67 season Spurs were assisted in their goals column by just one own goal. It came in a 2-0 win against Leicester City, and was scored by a player who had a happier experience in London ten years later when he captained Southampton to win the FA Cup in 1976. Who was he?

9. Although compared to the early 1960s they now had a problem scoring goals consistently, they could still be devastating on occasion. Which Lancastrian club went down 5-0 and 7-0 in the successive seasons of 1967/68 and 1968/69?

10. As the decade ended, Spurs were in the lowest position they had been in since the 1958/59 season, but the final game of 1969/70 brought some comfort with a 1-0 home win over Arsenal on 11 May 1970 that meant Spurs finished above them. Who got the winner?

QUIZ No. 50

SPURS IN THE FOOTBALL LEAGUE – THE 1970s

1. Three Spurs players, in 1970/71, appeared in all 42 league matches for the club. One was the main man up front, while the other two shared midfield duties and the first letters of their surnames. Who were the three players?

2. Which player was Spurs' top scorer in the league for 1976/77 despite not reaching double figures?

3. An Alan Gilzean goal gave Spurs a 1-1 draw at Boothferry Park, the home of Hull City, on 25 August 1971. However, Hull City were not in the First Division, so why were Spurs playing a game there?

4. It's very rare for someone to score four goals from midfield. It's even rarer when it comes away from home. It's beyond rare when it occurs at Old Trafford. Who performed this feat in a 4-1 Spurs win on 28 October 1972?

5. 1973/74 saw the only season in the club's history when their results took what statistical formation?

6. 1974/75 brought a few worrying signs that unfortunately came to fruition with relegation two years down the line. The season's league highlight was a 5-2 win at Newcastle United on 11 January 1975 when which Spurs player claimed his only hat-trick for the club?

7. 1975/76 brought a temporary improvement to reach ninth place, and the arrival on the scene of Glenn Hoddle. One Spurs player appeared in all 84 league games over season 1975/76 and 1976/77. Chelsea had their flashier version but Spurs their own reliable alternative. Who was he?

8. Relegation finally overtook Spurs in 1976/77 when they finished bottom of Division One. They did, however, win 12 games, which was a better haul than how many other clubs?

9. Spurs scrambled back to the top flight in the 1977/78 season. Bolton went up as champions and Spurs went up on goal difference in third spot, sandwiched between two teams from the south coast, one of which went up with them while the other lost out. Who were the two teams?

10. In 1978/79 Spurs introduced their Argentinian duo. They had a tough start but eventually things turned out brilliantly. Who scored the most league goals in that first season, Ossie Ardiles or Ricky Villa?

QUIZ No. 51

SPURS IN THE FOOTBALL LEAGUE – THE 1980s

1. Which new Spurs signing from Stoke City hit the ground running by scoring in each of his first three games, and registering a hat-trick in a 4-2 win over Crystal Palace at White Hart Lane on 12 November 1980?

2. Which club in the 1980/81 season was the only one that Spurs drew 0-0 with twice in the league?

3. Spurs' new West stand was opened by Sir Stanley Rous on 6 February 1982, and the home team produced a performance worthy of the occasion by beating which Midlands club 6-1?

4. Which Tottenham defender failed by just one goal to be their joint top goalscorer in the league in 1982/83?

5. Over the decade six players were top scorer in a season for Spurs. They were Steve Archibald, Garth Crooks, Mark Falco, Clive Allen, Chris Waddle and Gary Lineker. Which one of these was top scorer in three seasons?

6. Spurs were a bit crazy where goals were concerned in 1985/86 when they managed to go six successive games without scoring, but also scored five times in a game on no fewer than six occasions. The six clubs they beat were Southampton, QPR, West Bromwich Albion, Oxford United, Sheffield Wednesday and Newcastle United. Five of these games were at White Hart Lane, but which one of the six clubs lost 5-2 at home to Spurs?

7. In 1986/87 Clive Allen scored exactly 11 times as many league goals as Paul Allen. How many did each of them score?

8. In 1987/88, Spurs scored just 38 goals in their 40 league games, which constituted the lowest total in their history, before or since. True or false?

9. Paul Stewart scored a hat-trick when Spurs won 5-0 away on 29 April 1989 against another London club. Which one?

10. This central defender came from Nottingham Forest and left for Leeds United after 60 league games for Spurs. In the 1987/88 season he was the only Spurs player to appear in all 40 league games. Who was he?

QUIZ No. 52

SPURS IN THE FOOTBALL LEAGUE – THE 1990s

1. Which Spurs player opened the first season with a goal in a 3-1 win over Manchester City at White Hart Lane, and then, in the next home game, got all three goals as Derby County were beaten 3-0?

2. Who scored for Spurs in their first four league games of the 1991/92 season?

3. Which London club scored five goals at home to Spurs on 23 February 1991, but then conceded five to them on a different home ground on 21 September of the same year, but in the following season?

4. Teddy Sheringham was the only player to score a league hat-trick for Spurs in the 1992/93 season, when they beat which club 4-0 at White Hart Lane on 20 February 1993?

5. Spurs flirted with relegation in the 1993/94 season. It didn't look likely when they won 5-0 at White Hart Lane on 18 September 1993, but when they played the same team away from home on 5 May 1994 they could not afford to lose or they would have been in big trouble with one game to go. Everyone could breathe a little easier when they emerged with a 2-0 win to preserve their Premier League status against which Lancastrian opponents?

6. The 1994/95 season began with a thrilling 4-3 away win in Yorkshire, and a great goal from the latest quality recruit arriving at the club. Who was he, and which team did Spurs beat?

7. Who scored for Spurs against Liverpool at White Hart Lane in a 2-0 win on 31 October 1992, and then, as a Liverpool player, scored for Spurs again by putting through his own net in a 1-1 draw at Anfield two years later on 26 November 1994?

8. Who, on 28 December 1998, scored a hat-trick for Spurs against Everton in a 4-1 win at White Hart Lane?

9. Not for the first or last time, Spurs had a field day against Southampton in the 1999/2000 season, running out 7-2 winners at White Hart Lane. One of their goals came from an own goal by a player who was shortly to join Spurs. Who was he?

10. During the decade five players were on the pitch for every game in at least one season. They were Teddy Sheringham, Ian Walker, Stephen Carr, Sol Campbell and Steve Sedgley. Only two of them did this in two seasons. Which two players?

QUIZ No. 53

SPURS IN EUROPE - THE 1960s

1. The club's first taste of European football came in season 1961/62 in which tournament?

2. On 13 September 1961, they must have wondered what they had let themselves in for when they went 4-0 down in the first leg in Poland. Some honour was restored when the match ended in a 4-2 defeat to which club?

3. The second leg produced a famous night under the lights at White Hart Lane as Spurs tore the Polish champions apart. By what score did they win that night and who scored a hat-trick?

4. In the next round they met, in Feyenoord, a team they were to do battle with, supporters as well, a number of times in the future. They beat them 4-2 on aggregate on this occasion. Which Spurs player, after the second Feyenoord match, had scored in all four matches in Europe thus far?

5. After victory over a tough Dukla Prague outfit, they reached the semi-final, where, after a pulsating second leg at White Hart Lane, they were very unlucky to go out 4-3 on aggregate to the eventual winners of the competition. Who were they?

6. 1962/63 saw them in the European Cup Winners' Cup, and straight away they were pitched against British opposition, prevailing 8-4 on aggregate. Who did they beat?

7. After two visits to Eastern Europe that accounted for Slovan Bratislava and O.F.K. Belgrade, they turned in a legendary performance in the final to beat Atletico Madrid by what score?

8. That victory meant that they were the first British club to win a European trophy, and when they defended it the following season they were in mouth-watering competition with another English club. Which one?

9. After two exciting hard-fought encounters, Spurs went down 4-3 on aggregate, but worse than that, which Spurs player broke his leg in the away fixture?

10. It was 1967/68 before Spurs experienced Europe again when, after beating Hadjuk Split, they went out on that frustrating system of the away goals rule. Which French club were the beneficiaries of the rule?

QUIZ No. 54

SPURS IN EUROPE – THE 1970s

1. The 1970s started really well for Spurs in Europe when they won the UEFA Cup in 1971/72. They started out against an Icelandic club called Keflavik, winning 6-1 away and 9-0 at home. A close-run thing! A different Spurs player scored a hat-trick in each game. Who were the two men?

2. After a 1-0 aggregate win over French club Nantes in the second round, they got off to a flyer when a goal inside 20 seconds against the appropriately named Rapid Bucharest helped them on their way to a 5-0 aggregate win in the third round. The same Spurs midfielder got the winner against Nantes and the super-quick goal against Rapid. Who was he?

3. Which Italian club did Spurs meet in the semi-final?

4. Despite significant spoiling tactics, Spurs won through to the final 3-2 on aggregate. Which midfielder's two goals in the first leg win at White Hart Lane were vital?

5. The final itself was against another First Division club in Wolves. Spurs won the away leg 2-1 with two Martin Chivers goals, but struggled to finish the job at White Hart Lane, drawing 1-1 on the night with a brave header from which midfield player who was knocked out in the process of scoring it?

6. Spurs defended their trophy the following season. In the quarter-final the away-goals rule worked for them against Vittoria Setubal, but the opposite happened against which English side in the semi-final when Spurs were beaten on away goals?

7. They didn't know it at the time, but 1973/74 was to be their last season in Europe in that decade. In the first round of the UEFA Cup that season they won 9-2 on aggregate against a Swiss team whose name suggested they were well fitted to play football, but the score suggested otherwise! Who were they?

8. Which Scottish club did Spurs beat 5-2 on aggregate in the second round that year?

9. Dinamo Tbilisi, I.F.C. Cologne and Locomotiv Leipzig were all beaten as Spurs reached their third European final. The first leg at White Hart Lane finished 2-2. One of the Spurs goals was an own goal. Who scored their other goal, and which team did they play in the final?

10. On 29 May 1974 Spurs lost the second leg 2-0, and with it their 100 per cent record in European finals. But what overshadowed the actual result?

QUIZ No. 55

SPURS IN EUROPE - THE 1980s

1. In the 1981/82 European Cup Winners' Cup Spurs were drawn against a side that had won the European Cup three times in a row in the 1970s, but any concerns were needless as the Londoners won 6-1 on aggregate against which club?

2. If it proved to be easy against triple European Champions in the first round it was anything but against Irish opposition in the next round. When they went through on aggregate 2-1 with two Garth Crooks goals, who did they beat?

3. Eintracht Frankfurt, whose 1960 European Cup Final against Real Madrid springs to mind whenever their name is mentioned, were beaten in the quarter-final, before Spurs went out 2-1 on aggregate in the semi-final to the eventual winners of the trophy. Who were they?

4. Who, at White Hart Lane on 7 April 1982, scored Tottenham's only goal over the two legs of the semi-final, in a 1-1 draw?

5. In the European Cup Winners' Cup of the following season, Spurs accounted for another Irish club in the first round. This time it was Coleraine, who lost 7-0 on aggregate. Who was the only Spurs player to score in both legs?

6. This time Spurs failed to get past the second round when, after a 1-1 home draw with Bayern Munich, they lost the second leg 4-1. Who scored their goal in Germany?

7. Spurs won the UEFA Cup in memorable fashion in 1983/84, but in the first round they swatted aside yet another Irish club, in this instance Drogheda United. Spurs didn't concede over the two games, but certainly scored a few goals. How many?

8. After Drogheda United, Spurs knocked out five more clubs in order to stand the UEFA Cup trophy on the sideboard at White Hart Lane. The following six clubs include the five they beat plus one impostor – Austria Vienna, Benfica, Hadjuk Split, Bayern Munich, Feyenoord and Anderlecht. Who shouldn't be there?

9. Who scored for Spurs in the away leg of the final, which ended in a 1-1 draw?

10. The same score prevailed in the final's second leg at White Hart Lane, and when extra-time failed to settle the issue it was decided by penalties. Whose goalkeeping heroics won the cup for Spurs and holds a special place in Spurs' history?

QUIZ No. 56

SPURS IN EUROPE – THE 1990s AND 2000s

1. It was disappointing fare for Spurs in Europe in the 1990s. After their usual FA Cup win with a 'one' at the end of the year in 1991, they entered the European Cup Winners' Cup for 1991/92. After beating Stockerau, Hadjuk Split and Porto, which old foe knocked them out?

2. Goals were the problem. They failed to score in their last three games in the tournament, managing just seven in eight matches. Who was their top scorer in Europe with three of those seven?

3. It was the end of the decade before Spurs got into Europe again, 1999/2000 to be precise, although we can dispense with the 2000 part straight away as Spurs only lasted until 4 November when they went out over two legs to Kaiserslautern in the second round of the UEFA Cup. Earlier, they had beaten Zimbru Chisinau 3-0 at White Hart Lane, before a 0-0 draw at their place, wherever that was, sent them through. In the White Hart Lane leg, Tim Sherwood got one goal, while the other two came from Spurs players with Wimbledon connections. Who were they?

4. The UEFA Cup is like pulling teeth! Perish the thought of having to qualify in July. You could easily die before you reached the competition proper. In 2006/07 Spurs had the dubious distinction of being back in Europe and became part of the appropriately named Group B, because all their opponents had that letter prominent in their names. They were Besiktas, Brugge, Bayer Leverkusen and Dinamo Bucharest. Also appropriately, which Spurs player scored in all four games?

5. Their next opponents were another 'B' in Braga. Spurs beat them 3-2 both home and away to advance to the quarter-final. Which Spurs midfielder scored in both legs?

6. Spurs lost that quarter-final 4-3 on aggregate to Seville, the eventual winners. At White Hart Lane in the second leg, which finished 2-2, it was galling that one of the visitors' goals was scored by an ex-Spur. Who was he?

7. Spurs were back in the UEFA Cup again in 2007/08, and knocked out a Czech side they had beaten in the previous season before the group stage. Who were they?

8. However, the dreaded penalty shoot-out did for them in the second knock out stage, when which club beat them 6-5 on penalties after a 1-1 aggregate score?

9. 2008/09 saw Spurs back again, this time in Group D. Their most encouraging performance was a 4-0 win over Dinamo Zagreb in which a Spurs player scored a hat-trick. Who was he?

10. In the so called 'round of 32', Spurs made their exit, beaten 3-1 on aggregate at the hands of which Ukrainian club?

QUIZ No. 57

SPURS IN EUROPE – THE 2010s – CLUBS

1. In the Champions League of 2010/11, Spurs beat two teams from the same city. Which one?

2. In the disappointing Europa League campaign of 2011/12, Spurs qualified for the group stage by beating a Scottish club 5-0 on aggregate in a play-off, but didn't get out of the group despite winning three of their six games, including two against an Irish club. Who were the Scottish and Irish clubs involved here?

3. In 2012/13, Spurs went out of the same competition to Basel on penalties in the quarter-final, but, in the group stage, which Italian club drew with them 0-0 in both matches?

4. Which club knocked Spurs out of the Europa League at the round-of-16 stage in season 2013/14 by 5-3 on aggregate before going on to be beaten in the final by Seville on penalties?

5. Which Italian club did Spurs face in the round of 32 in the Europa League in both 2014/15 and 2015/16, losing on the first occasion, but winning on the second?

6. When Spurs started playing their Champions League games at Wembley in 2016/17, they were not very successful, losing two and winning one of their group games. It was the final game that produced a 3-1 win, but it didn't lead to qualification. Which Russian club did they beat?

7. They were then shunted into the Europa League halfway through that competition, one of the many idiocies that UEFA has produced down the years. That adventure lasted one round when they lost 3-2 on aggregate to which Belgian club?

8. Who were the only club to play Spurs in this decade in Europe that had met them previously in a European final?

9. 2018/19 produced a wonderful season of Champions League football when Spurs looked dead and buried on more than one occasion before coming up smelling of roses! Then, in the semi-final, it really did look all over for them when a sensational Lucas Moura hat-trick transformed a 0-2 score line in their favour against which club?

10. 2019/20 brought a reality check as Spurs set a new record they didn't want concerning the number of goals conceded at home in a group game. After fighting back from that experience, they went out tamely in the first knockout stage. Two German clubs inflicted the damage. Who were they?

QUIZ No. 58

SPURS IN EUROPE - THE 2010s - PLAYERS

1. In 2010/11, Spurs had to qualify for the Champions League by playing a team that sounded like they wouldn't put up much of a fight! They were Young Boys of Berne. But when Spurs visited Switzerland, they found themselves 3-0 down inside half an hour. After their eventual 3-2 defeat, they put things right in the second leg with a 4-0 win at White Hart Lane. Who scored a hat-trick in that game for Spurs?

2. Spurs played some great football in Europe that season, scoring 18 goals in their six group games, before finding it much harder to score in the latter stages of the campaign. Particularly memorable were two games with Inter Milan. Whose brilliant second-half hat-trick when Spurs were 4-0 down away from home in the first leg made people sit up and take notice of his talents?

3. In the Europa League of 2012/13, Spurs beat Maribor 3-1 at White Hart Lane and qualified for the round of 32 where a last-minute goal in Lyon turned defeat into victory. They finally went out in the quarter-final on penalties to Basel after two 2-2 draws. Three players starting with a 'D' were involved. The first got a hat-trick against Maribor, the second got the late and vital goal in Lyon, while the third got both goals in the away leg against Basel. Who were the three players?

4. He was much maligned on occasion, but he came good in the last group match at White Hart Lane in the Europa League of 2013/14. Spurs defeated a team 4-0, who only gave trouble to the programme compiler in making sure he had spelt Anzhi Makhachkala correctly! Who got three of the Spurs goals?

5. In 2015/16, in the last Europa League group stage match, whose hat-trick helped Spurs overcome Monaco 4-1 at White Hart Lane?

6. That same Monaco side ruined Spurs' first European night at Wembley in the Champions League of 2016/17 by winning 2-1. Which player scored Spurs' first Wembley Champions League goal that night?

7. Who is the only player to score a hat-trick for Spurs in both the Champions League and the Europa League?

8. Apart from the awful let down at the end when Liverpool had the look of a team that could be beaten after a hard season if only Spurs had turned up, the Champions League run of 2018/19 brought many heart-stopping moments that would not be easily forgotten. Losing two and drawing one of your first three group games usually spells disaster, and even though they rallied, all looked lost when the last group game in Barcelona moved into its last five minutes. Whose goal changed all that?

9. More excitement was to follow when Spurs were in a bad way in the second leg of the quarter-final at Manchester City. But, riding their luck, they came up with a killer goal right at the death that transformed the night and left City in despair. Who got it?

10. At times, the Champions League of 2019/20 was a chastening experience. Spurs eventually went out at the first knockout stage, but not before a few stirring performances. During this campaign, three Spurs players scored their first goal in Europe for the club. The first came in a 4-0 away win against Red Star Belgrade, the second in a 4-2 home win over Olympiakos, and the last in a 3-1 defeat at Bayern Munich. Who were the three goalscorers?

QUIZ No. 59

SPURS IN THE SOUTHERN LEAGUE – 1896-1908

Multiple choice

1. Spurs began their first season of Southern League football in 1896/97 with three consecutive away games before they played and lost their first home game on 10 October 1896. Who beat them?
    (a) Chatham (b) Reading (c) Swindon Town (d) Millwall Athletic

2. One club that Spurs met in every Southern League season they played in were New Brompton. What name do they go by now?
    (a) Oxford United (b) Bristol Rovers (c) Gillingham (d) Southend

3. In their 12 seasons of Southern League football Spurs finished runners-up twice but had one season when they won it. Which season was it?
    (a) 1898/99 (b) 1899/1900 (c) 1900/01 (d) 1901/02

4. Which team did Spurs beat 7-0 and 8-1 at home in the 1901 calendar year?
    (a) Portsmouth (b) Brentford (c) West Ham United (d) Watford

5. In season 1901/02, which club did Spurs play five times, twice in the league and three times in the FA Cup without beating them?
    (a) Northampton Town (b) Luton Town (c) Southampton
    (d) Wellingborough

6. In 1903/04, Spurs endured a terrible first half of the season when they won just three of their first 15 games but were so good in the second half that they eventually finished second. They created an unwanted club record by failing to score from the start of the season for how many games?
    (a) Four (b) Five (c) Six (d) Seven

7. Spurs played their first Southern League fixture on their new White Hart Lane ground on 9 September 1899. Which club did they beat 1-0?
    (a) QPR (b) Brighton (c) Bristol City (d) Thames Ironworks

8. Who was the only player to score over 50 league goals for Spurs in the 12 seasons of Southern League membership?
(a) Sandy Brown (b) John Cameron (c) Jack Kirwan
(d) David Copeland

9. Four top players for Spurs in their Southern League days were two Sandys, Brown and Tait, and two Toms, Pratt and Smith. All of them had previously played for which Lancastrian club?
(a) Blackburn Rovers (b) Burnley (c) Preston North End
(d) Bolton Wanderers

10. He was top scorer in their last Southern League season and in their first Football League season as well. Who was he?
(a) Bert Middlemiss (b) Vivian Woodward (c) Herbert Chapman
(d) Jimmy Pass

QUIZ No. 60

SPURS QUOTES

1. 'It's not the Yorkshire Ripper I'm signing.' Which Spurs manager said this and which player was he talking about?

2. 'I didn't know you were a Spurs fan.' Which opposition manager, who had been at Spurs himself briefly as a player, said this and to which referee after one of his decisions in a game against Spurs displeased him?

3. 'I thought he said, "Do you want to visit a brewery?"' Which Spurs player said this about which England manager with Spurs connections, and about what?

4. 'In my time at Tottenham I made lots of mistakes. The biggest was probably employing him.' Which Spurs chairman said this about which Spurs manager?

5. 'A few idiots have adorned my house in Middlesbrough with rotten eggs. There was also a murder threat in the mailbox.' Which player said this on his move to Spurs?

6. 'No one at Tottenham would shed a single tear if he was sacked tomorrow. The dressing room is not together and there is no team spirit. He has absolutely no management skills.' Which Spurs player gave this ringing endorsement and about which manager?

7. 'We looked all around Europe for people with any credentials, but it is a fact that anyone who is any good was already tied up with a job.' Some employers can make a new manager feel like a million dollars. Which new manager has Alan Sugar made feel he's worth about a dollar fifty?

8. 'I won two FA Cups and two UEFA Cups with Tottenham, but I never jumped as high as when I heard that draw.' Which ex-Spurs player, now a director of which club, said this upon learning that his team has drawn Manchester United in the FA Cup?

9. 'I'm very pleased for him, but it's a bit like watching your mother-in-law drive off a cliff in your new car.' Which Spurs manager bemoans losing which star player to a foreign club?

10. 'I play football for money. You mustn't undersell yourself because you like the club. True relationships don't exist. It's not about friendship or camaraderie.' Which Spurs player from this century makes sure nobody wants his name on the back of their shirt?

QUIZ No. 61

SUPER SPURS - OSVALDO ARDILES

1. Eyebrows were raised when Spurs splashed out on two Argentinians at the start of the 1978/79 season, but Ricky Villa went down in Spurs folklore with that goal at Wembley, and Ossie Ardiles turned out to be quite simply one of the finest to ever wear a Spurs shirt. From which Argentinian club was he signed? They sound like the effect he produced at White Hart Lane!

2. He took a while to get that elusive first goal, but when it arrived on 3 March 1979 he got an extra one for good measure in a 2-0 home win over which club?

3. The following week, on 10 March, he scored his first Spurs goal in an FA Cup tie that ended in a 1-1 draw at White Hart Lane, with Spurs going out in the replay. The same team came to Spurs in the third round of the next season and again Ardiles scored in another 1-1 draw. This time, though, Spurs turned in a great performance in the replay, winning 1-0 after extra time, and it was Ardiles again who got the vital goal. Which club did he score these three FA Cup goals against?

4. Ossie scored twice for Spurs in Europe, firstly in the European Cup Winners' Cup in September 1981 at White Hart Lane, and secondly in the UEFA Cup in an away tie in March 1984. The first came against a household cleaner, and the other came against a combination of a country and the capital city. Who were the two clubs he scored against?

5. Ardiles scored in the league two years running in Spurs wins of 2-0 and 3-1 in January 1981 and March 1982 on the ground of which south-coast club?

6. After winning an FA Cup winner's medal when Spurs beat Manchester City in 1981, why wasn't Ossie running around Wembley with another winner's medal the following year when they beat QPR?

7. Ardiles twice left White Hart Lane. Which two clubs widely known by acronyms did he join?

8. After his playing career ended, he had a spell as manager of Spurs, trying to create an exciting, attacking team in his image, but ended up getting the sack. Which three other English clubs did he manage?

9. Ossie was mentioned in Tottenham's song that celebrated their FA Cup Final appearance in 1981, when it was alleged that 'his knees have gone all trembly'. Who performed the song?

10. Ardiles was already a World Cup winner when he joined Spurs. The club had already had one World Cup winner join them previously, and another came in the 1990s before, finally, they had a player win one while he was at the club. Who were the three players?

QUIZ No. 62

SUPER SPURS – DANNY BLANCHFLOWER

1. With which Irish club did Danny Blanchflower start his career in football?

2. When he arrived in this country and asked for a ball in training, he was told that it wasn't allowed because if the players didn't see one during the week it made them hungrier for it on a Saturday! Which Yorkshire club gave him his start in English football?

3. His next move was to a big club in the Midlands that had been underachieving for some time. Which one?

4. It was ironic that for someone so committed to attacking football his first game for Spurs ended in a 0-0 draw away to which northern club?

5. Which product did he advertise on television in the 1950s in a clip that showed him swerving around two tackles in the green of Northern Ireland? Obviously, it didn't look so green on black-and-white TV!

6. A real thinker about the game and a captain who took it upon himself to change things if they weren't going well, when asked what his footballing philosophy was, what, with a little bit of blarney, was his reply?

7. His inspiring leadership and tactical acumen were major factors in Northern Ireland's performance in the 1958 World Cup in Sweden. What stage of the tournament did they reach?

8. After leading Spurs to the double in 1960/61, the following season saw him score with two penalties in key moments of two different cup competitions against teams beginning with 'B'. Who were they?

9. He could be difficult. Which host of the television programme *This Is Your Life* was rebuffed when Danny didn't think much of being the subject of the show?

10. His first Spurs goal came at White Hart Lane in August 1956 and contributed to a 5-2 Spurs win. His last Spurs goal came in November 1962 in a 4-0 win on the same ground. The beaten clubs both began with an 'L'. Who were they?

QUIZ No. 63

SUPER SPURS – JIMMY GREAVES

1. On which ground and against which club did Jimmy Greaves score the first league goal of his career on the first day of the 1957/58 season?

2. Which Italian club did he play for before he joined Spurs?

3. What was the fee Spurs paid to secure his services?

4. Typically, he scored a hat-trick on his league debut in a 5-2 win at White Hart Lane on 16 December 1961. Which northern club did Spurs beat that day?

5. If you've seen the clip of Jimmy and Bobby Moore doing a little dance together during a match between Spurs and West Ham United at White Hart Lane, you will have gathered that they were the best of mates. They share something else too. They made their England debuts against the same South American country. Jimmy's was in a 4-1 defeat in 1959, while Bobby's came in a 4-0 win in the same city in 1962, when Jimmy got a hat-trick. Which country was involved?

6. In 1962/63, Jimmy broke Tottenham's record for league goals in a season, a record that still stands. How many goals did he score in the 41 games he played in?

7. How many seasons in a row did he top the Spurs goalscoring charts, and who did he share the accolade with in his final season at the club?

8. Which player came to Spurs as part of the deal that took Jimmy to West Ham United in 1970?

9. Jimmy's last goal for Spurs came on 10 January 1970 in a 2-1 win at White Hart Lane against a team that share Spurs' colours. Who were they?

10. Of players who have scored more than 20 England goals, Jimmy has a better scoring rate than three Spurs men, Gary Lineker, Peter Crouch and Harry Kane. However, one Spurs player's record outstrips even Jimmy's 44 in 57 internationals. The man in question, who played for Spurs between 1901 and 1909, scored 29 goals in 23 games for England. Who was he?

QUIZ No. 64

SUPER SPURS - GLENN HODDLE

1. A silky-smooth creator, Glenn Hoddle came on as a substitute for his first Spurs outing on 30 August 1975 in a 2-2 draw at White Hart Lane against which club?

2. His first Spurs goal coincided with his first start when he beat Peter Shilton from distance in a 2-1 away win over which club?

3. Glenn scored just one goal in Europe for Spurs. It came on 17 March 1982 in a 2-1 defeat in Germany in the European Cup Winners' Cup. Who beat Spurs on that occasion?

4. He scored ten League Cup goals during his time at White Hart Lane, but only found the net twice in a single game on one occasion in a 5-3 second-leg win over which Yorkshire club on 8 October 1986?

5. Glenn Hoddle's total of 53 England caps should have been higher, but his skills were under appreciated. His first cap came at Wembley in a 2-0 European Championship win on 22 November 1979, when he scored one of the goals against which country from eastern Europe?

6. His only Spurs hat-trick came on 27 February 1980 in a 4-3 league win at White Hart Lane. Their opponents that day were also the team he scored the most goals against in his Spurs career. Which Midlands club were they?

7. Glenn Hoddle was top league goalscorer for Spurs with 19 goals, quite a feat for a midfielder, just once. In what season?

8. Which London club did he score against in three FA Cup matches in successive seasons?

9. Only two clubs have experienced Glenn Hoddle scoring against them in both the FA Cup and the League Cup. One is from the Midlands and the other is Welsh. Who are the two clubs?

10. After nearly 500 Tottenham games in all competitions, Glenn left White Hart Lane in July 1987 for which club?

QUIZ No. 65

SUPER SPURS - PAT JENNINGS

1. Which Irish club did Pat Jennings play for before he came to England?

2. His contemporary and fellow international goalkeeper Ray Clemence had some similarities with Pat. They both won the FA Cup with Spurs, they both played for three English clubs, and both played 48 times for their first club. Ray's was Scunthorpe United. What was Pat's?

3. Pat Jennings played in two League Cup finals and one FA Cup Final for Spurs. Who was the only man to score against him in those three matches?

4. On 12 August 1967 in a 3-3 draw in the Charity Shield against Manchester United at Old Trafford, one of Pat's clearances ended up in United's net. Which goalkeeper has probably seen it on TV a few times from behind an armchair?

5. Pat Jennings, between 1964 and 1986, made 119 appearances in goal for Northern Ireland. Among goalkeepers from England, Scotland, Wales and the Irish Republic, who are the only two to have played more times for their country?

6. What did Pat do at Anfield against Liverpool on 31 March 1973 that is not often seen?

7. Pat Jennings is unique among goalkeepers in having won both the FWA and PFA 'Footballer of the Year' awards. Only four other goalkeepers have won either of these awards. Who are they?

8. Pat Jennings is high on the Tottenham appearances list, having played in 472 league games for the club. If they hadn't let him leave in 1977 he may well have been number one. The closest goalkeeper to him played 418 games for Spurs. Who was he?

9. I've already suggested links between the careers of Pat Jennings and Ray Clemence. Between them, overall, not just for Spurs, they played over 1,500 league games. Incredibly, they can be separated by just one game, Pat playing in 757 matches. Did Ray Clemence play 756 or 758?

10. Some Spurs fans might not have approved of Pat's inclusion in my 'Super Spurs' category because of his Arsenal association. My view is that it was the club's fault and while it would have been preferable for his 'Indian Summer' to have taken place elsewhere, he's entitled to work where he's wanted. Pat played in three FA Cup finals for Arsenal and one for Spurs. In those he played with and against 68 men, but only one of them shared the first letter of his surname with Pat. Who was he?

QUIZ No. 66

SUPER SPURS - CLIFF JONES

1. Brave as a lion, quick as a hare, effective on either wing and great in the air, Cliff Jones tearing down the wing was a sight to behold for Spurs fans, and his career coincided with the greatest period in the club's history. Strangely enough, Cliff played for two other league clubs and didn't need to change his colours. Who were they?

2. How much did Spurs pay for him in 1958, which was a record for a winger at that time?

3. His debut has been covered elsewhere, but against which Midlands club did he score his first Spurs goal in a 3-1 away win on 19 April 1958?

4. Here's a tough one! On 3 April 1963, Cliff scored his only hat-trick for Wales in a 4-1 away win in the Home International Championship against Northern Ireland. The Welsh team that day had a fellow Spur in it who played over 200 times for the club. It also contained a man who wasn't yet at Spurs, but soon would be a major addition to their defence. Who were the two Welshmen?

5. The beaten Northern Ireland team on that memorable day for Cliff Jones contained a future Spurs manager. Who was he?

6. In how many seasons did Cliff Jones reach double figures in goals for Spurs in the league?

7. His 135 league goals from the wing is a real tribute to his finishing ability, never mind the rest of his game. Not many wingers finished their careers with those stats. In fact, only one member of the double side scored more than Cliff and the latter made a good few of those for him. Who was he?

8. Which club did he score five FA Cup goals against in three matches over the 1959/60 and 1960/61 seasons?

9. Cliff was a proud member of a heroic Welsh side that reached the World Cup quarter-final in Sweden in 1958. He played in all five games, in the last of which they gave the eventual winners a scare before a goal from Pele sent Brazil through. Which Tottenham player scored the winner in a play-off with Hungary to ensure they progressed in the tournament in an earlier game?

10. What employment was Cliff Jones engaged in after his illustrious career came to an end?

QUIZ No. 67

SUPER SPURS - ROBBIE KEANE

1. The phrase 'well-travelled' could have been invented for Robbie Keane, but he had that knack of making things happen out of nothing, and fans loved his trademark goal celebration. He was a real handful for defenders from the age of 17 onwards and ended up scoring in the Premier League for six clubs: Spurs and which five others?

2. Who is currently the only player to have bettered this by scoring for seven?

3. Along the way he turned out for an Italian club, a Scottish club and an American club. Who were they?

4. Spurs signed him in 2002, the first of two spells for the club. Which Spurs manager signed him, from which club, and how much did he cost?

5. After scoring a hat-trick against Everton in 2002/03, he got another the following season, and this time it was against one of his former clubs. Who were his victims on this occasion?

6. In 2003/04 when Arsenal came to White Hart Lane to celebrate their title on the last day of the season, he spoilt their day slightly by scoring from the spot to gain Spurs a 2-2 draw near the end of a game they had always looked likely to lose. He had won the penalty himself by standing on the Arsenal goalkeeper's foot at a corner, which produced a retaliatory shove. Who was the goalkeeper?

7. Robbie set a Spurs record by reaching double figures in Premier League goals in how many successive seasons?

8. In a messy transfer, he joined Liverpool in July 2008. However, six months later, his return to White Hart Lane caused which company to use this advert: 'Liverpool to London returns faster than Robbie Keane'?

9. Not content with England, Scotland, Italy and America, on 4 August 2017, Robbie signed for Indian Super League club A.T.K. Perhaps it had something to do with the man with Spurs connections who was head coach at A.T.K. at the time. Who was he?

10. Robbie Keane's international record for the Irish Republic is very impressive indeed. Top goalscorer with 68 in a staggering 146 games, he holds a unique record in international football that encompasses his 19 years on that stage. What is it?

QUIZ No. 68

SUPER SPURS – LEDLEY KING

1. In a one-club career that would have produced over 500 games for Spurs without a permanently dodgy left knee that he showed great courage to overcome, Ledley King's debut for Spurs came in a 3-2 defeat on a famous ground on 1 May 1999 when he came on as a substitute. Which ground?

2. Which Spurs manager gave him his opportunity?

3. He scored ten goals in 268 league games for Spurs, but his first was the most memorable as it went into the record books as the fastest Premier League goal, measured at 9.82 seconds. It came in a 3-3 away draw against which club?

4. That record stood for over 18 years before someone scored a faster one on 23 April 2019. Who was it?

5. Many opponents, including Thierry Henry, have commented on Ledley's effortless qualities as a reader of the game, and on the timing of his tackles. The fact that he didn't often have to resort to fouling the opposition is borne out by the number of yellow cards he received in his career. Was that number less than ten or not?

6. Ledley was not only unlucky with injuries, he was also unfortunate that his career partially coincided with those of Tony Adams and John Terry. Nevertheless, he represented England 21 times, the first of those caps coming on 27 March 2002 in Yorkshire. Who were England's opponents and on which ground was the match played?

7. One other Spurs player was in that England team. Who was it?

8. Ledley scored two goals for England, one coming in a 1-1 away draw with Portugal in 2004, while the other arrived at Wembley in a 3-1 win over which South American country in 2010?

9. Ledley King's first FA Cup goal for Spurs came in a 4-0 win in the fifth round at White Hart Lane on 17 February 2001 against which Lancastrian club?

10. Ledley's only League Cup goal came in Tottenham's first match on the way to the final in Cardiff in 2001/02. Which club from the South West were beaten 2-0 at White Hart Lane?

QUIZ No. 69

SUPER SPURS - GARY MABBUTT

1. Gary Mabbutt ran through walls in the Spurs defence for 16 years, 11 of them as an inspiring captain despite health problems with diabetes that would have stopped a lesser man. Playing a bit further forward than the position he later occupied, he scored for Spurs in his very first game at the start of the 1982/83 season at White Hart Lane against which club?

2. Before he joined Spurs he played 131 games for a club that his father played for in over three times that total. Which club?

3. Gary scored at both ends in the 1987 FA Cup Final between Spurs and Coventry City, his own goal being particularly cruel because it came from his heroic effort to stop a goal. Only two players had previously scored at both ends in an FA Cup Final. One is covered elsewhere as Spurs were involved, but who became the first player to do it in the 1946 FA Cup Final between Charlton Athletic and Derby County?

4. Gary scored an FA Cup goal against just one London club in a 4-0 home win in the fourth round on 31 January 1987. He also scored just one League Cup goal against a different London club in a 2-0 home win in the third round on 6 November 1985. Who were the two London clubs who, incidentally, have shared a ground? Hope that helps!

5. Which Irish club did Gary score twice against in a 6-0 away win in the UEFA Cup of 1983/84?

6. Gary made his England debut at Wembley on 13 October 1982 in a 2-1 defeat in a friendly against which country?

7. His only England goal came on 12 November 1986 in a European Championship match at Wembley when England won 2-0 against a country that no longer exists. Who were they?

8. Whose 'challenge' on Gary Mabbutt in a game at White Hart Lane between Spurs and Wimbledon caused him to sustain a fractured eye socket and a fractured skull, necessitating the wearing of a mask years before they became de rigueur in 2020?

9. On the opening day of the 1996/97 season, Spurs won 2-0 away, but there was little joy in that for Gary Mabbutt who suffered a broken leg in the game that effectively ended his career, despite a brave comeback the following year. The ground this accident happened on was the same ground that Bobby Moore played his final league game on. What ground was it?

10. Gary got on the pitch 11 times in the following league season, but was forced to call it a day on 10 May 1998 in a 1-1 draw against which south-coast club at White Hart Lane?

QUIZ No. 70

SUPER SPURS - DAVE MACKAY

1. My idea of the greatest of all Spurs players came to the club in 1959, making his debut against which team in a 3-1 win at White Hart Lane on 21 March of that year?

2. On successive Saturdays of 12 and 19 September 1959, Dave Mackay scored in 5-1 wins over two Lancastrian clubs, one away and one at home. Who were they?

3. Dave Mackay got his only Spurs hat-trick against which London club on 22 December 1962?

4. In 1964 Dave Mackay suffered two broken legs, the second of them coming in his first game back in the reserves at White Hart Lane against which club?

5. On 20 August 1966, as the curtain came up on a new season, Spurs beat Leeds United 3-1 at White Hart Lane. A photograph that became well known in football circles shows an incident from the game where Dave Mackay is holding another player by the throat! Who was that Leeds United player that Dave was introducing himself to, and, for bonus points, who is the other Spurs player in the picture, and who is the referee running with whistle to his lips like a fire engine coming to put out a fire?

6. In that season Dave Mackay scored home and away against a club from the North East as Spurs won 4-0 and 2-0. Who were they?

7. Dave Mackay's last Spurs goal came on 20 April 1968 at White Hart Lane in a 4-2 win over which Midlands club?

8. Which manager lured Dave Mackay away from Spurs in 1968 to be his central defender and voice on the pitch, and which club did he sign for?

9. After a superb season in 1968/69 when his astute footballing brain helped his tiring body out to the extent that he won promotion and missed just one league game of the 42, he was Footballer of the Year at the season's end. In fact, he had to share the award with a Manchester City player who was also doing great things in the veteran stage of his career. Who was he?

10. Dave Mackay is a member of a select group of nine men that includes Bill Nicholson. What have members of this group achieved?

QUIZ No. 71

SUPER SPURS - BILL NICHOLSON

1. Known as 'Mr. Tottenham', Bill Nicholson gave the best part of his life to Spurs, spending as much time at White Hart Lane as he did in his house a few yards from the ground. Tottenham's greatest manager came from Scarborough and biographical accounts often refer to him as a dour Yorkshireman. Only one Yorkshireman since Bill has managed the club. Who was he?

2. A one-club man, Bill joined Spurs as a player in 1938 and but for the war would have probably added another 200 or so appearances to the 342 he accumulated in all competitions. A defensive-minded wing-half, he scored just six goals for Spurs, and they all came in the league. He scored against Nottingham Forest, Bury, Huddersfield Town and three London clubs in close geographical proximity. Who were they?

3. Bill's solitary international appearance has been dealt with elsewhere, but on which northern club ground did it take place?

4. Bill Nicholson was a key member of the 1950/51 'push and run' side that won the league for the first time in the club's history. How many of the 42 games did Bill miss?

5. His first match in charge of Spurs became the stuff of legend and has been covered elsewhere, but which three of the 11 that lined up for Spurs on 11 October 1958 were in the famous double-winning side of 1960/61?

6. When Bill signed for Spurs in 1938, he did so on the same day as another player who came from Wales and also became part of the 1950/51 champions. Bill Nicholson always said he was the most important player in all his time at the club. Who was he?

7. Complete this expression of Bill's with four more words. 'When the ball goes dead ...'

8. Bill managed Spurs to three FA Cup wins in the 1960s. Since World War One only two other clubs had won the FA Cup three times in a decade, one in the 1920s and the other in the 1950s. Who were they?

9. Bill won the league as a player and a manager. He was only the second person to do so. Who, in 1955, was the first and which man with Spurs connections joined Bill in doing it in 1962?

10. Bill's resignation was a sad moment in the history of the club. In August of 1974, sickened by what he had witnessed in Rotterdam, fed up with the demands of modern players, and disillusioned with the way football was going, Bill decided his time was up. Spurs had made their worst start to a season for 62 years, losing their first four games. They had lost twice to Manchester City and had been beaten by a side whose only season in the top flight before or since was that of 1974/75. Who were they?

QUIZ No. 72

SUPER SPURS - STEVE PERRYMAN

1. A tireless midfield dynamo, Steve's Tottenham career spanned three decades, and his appearance record of 866 games in all competitions will never be beaten in today's football world. What an inspiration! But how many league games was he on the field for: 635, 645, 655 or 665?

2. His Spurs debut came on 27 September 1969 and his day was ruined by Spurs going down 1-0 at home to which club from the North East?

3. His first goal for Spurs came on Boxing Day of 1969 in a 2-0 home win over another London club. Strangely enough, Spurs beat the same opponents by the same score at the same venue the following season, and Steve scored in that game too. Who did Spurs beat?

4. Steve Perryman managed to score a pair of goals from midfield on three occasions in his Spurs career. The first came in the vital UEFA Cup semi-final home leg on 5 April 1972 and helped Spurs to go on to win the trophy. Which Italian club did his goals knock out of the competition?

5. The other two times he scored a brace of goals were more bread-and-butter affairs, and they both came at White Hart Lane in wins of 3-0 and 5-0 in March 1975 and the same month a year later, the first time against a Midlands club and the last against a Yorkshire club. Who were the two clubs?

6. Who were the only club that Steve Perryman scored against in both the league and the FA Cup?

7. Although he gained 17 'under-23' caps for England, he played somewhat less than that for the full England side, making his debut as a substitute in which cold city in 1982?

8. Which West Ham United player did he replace when he came on in that game?

9.   Which two other English league clubs did Steve Perryman play for after he left Spurs in March 1986?

10. As a manager he was at Watford between 1990 and 1993, and later managed more than one club in Japan, but in between he began a management career in Norway with a club with a very appropriate name for someone coming to a new job. Who were they?

TERRIFIC TIMES

1. Spurs registered a 9-2 win over this Midlands club at White Hart Lane on 29 September 1962, with Jimmy Greaves on the mark four times. He liked playing against them, getting a hat-trick in a 4-1 win in the following season? Who were they?

2. Which Spurs player hit the net five times at White Hart Lane on 22 November 2009 in a 9-1 win over Wigan Athletic?

3. Spurs' 10-4 win over Everton on 11 October 1958 has been covered elsewhere, so here's an off-the-wall question that ancient Spurs fans might be able to answer. Why did that particular score line resonate with people at that time?

4. Considering the 13-2 win over Crewe Alexandra in 1960 and the 9-1 win over Wigan Athletic in 2009, how many goals did Spurs score if you combine the best two 45-minute performances from those games?

5. On 21 November 1931, White Hart Lane experienced 12 goals in a Division Two game between Spurs and Port Vale. What was the score?

6. Spurs set their record for a league win when they beat which club 9-0 in a Division Two game at White Hart Lane on 22 October 1977?

7. Which club did Spurs beat 8-0 on 28 March 1936 in Division Two and 7-2 in the Premier League on 11 March 1999?

8. Which club did Spurs score seven times against in an away game that ended the 2016/17 Premier League season on 21 May 2017?

9. Spurs had struggled to draw 1-1 away to a club from the North West in the FA Cup third round on 10 January 1953. However, two days later they won the replay, a concept now consigned to the scrapheap, by 9-1. Who were their opponents?

10. On which two away grounds did Spurs score six goals in the Premier League, the first in April of 2017, and the second in December of 2018?

QUIZ No. 74

TOTTENHAM HOTSPUR – SEASON 2000/01

1. Despite finishing no higher than 12th, Spurs were not beaten at White Hart Lane in the league until which month?

2. Two sides came away from White Hart Lane with all three points during the season. If it helps, they also contested the 1970 FA Cup Final. Who were they?

3. Scoring 47 goals in 38 games is never going to win you much, and there was a run of successive 0-0 draws in January that extended to the start of the next month. How many 0-0 draws in a row were Spurs involved in?

4. Spurs managed four goals in the Premier League just once in 38 games. Let's hope that wasn't the day you had to go to a wedding! The goals came on 2 January for Anderton, Doherty, Rebrov and Ferdinand. Which team, beaten 4-2 at White Hart Lane, had a long journey home?

5. After accounting for Brentford after a replay in the League Cup, Spurs went out of the competition on home soil to another team from a lower division who knocked Spurs out on their way to a final that would have given Spurs fans their most amusing moment of the season! Who were they?

6. Who scored Spurs' only hat-trick in a Premier League game in a 3-0 home win over Leicester City on 25 November 2000?

7. Which Spurs defender was their only representative in the PFA Divisional Team of the year?

8. Who was leading goalscorer for Spurs over all competitions with 12?

9. Spurs' failure in the FA Cup semi-final is covered elsewhere, but on the way to that stage they knocked out three London clubs who are geographically close to each other. Who were the three?

10. The real moment of note that season came with Ledley King's record-breaking goal on 9 December 2000 that has been covered in his own section. In the 3-3 draw that day, the other goals for Spurs were scored by Chris Armstrong and which Spurs defender?

QUIZ No. 75

TOTTENHAM HOTSPUR – SEASON 2001/02

1. It is not usually a good sign when your goalkeeper picks up the club's 'Player of the Year' award. Which Spurs man won it in 2001/02?

2. A player that had his fair share of injuries while at Spurs was nevertheless the man who spent the most time on the pitch for them in the Premier League that season, starting 33 games and coming on in two more. Who was he?

3. It is relatively rare to play the same club in both the FA Cup and the League Cup in the same season. It is rarer still to do this against two clubs in the same season, and you would imagine it to be unheard of if you stretched it to three clubs. However, that is what happened to Spurs in 2001/02. Which three clubs were involved?

4. Six players scored for Spurs in the league and both cup competitions. Who is missing from the following list? Darren Anderton, Les Ferdinand, Steffen Iversen, Gustavo Poyet and Teddy Sheringham.

5. Anthony Barness, of Bolton Wanderers, performed an unwanted 'double' against Spurs in the domestic cup competitions. What was it?

6. Which two geographically close London clubs did Spurs knock out of the League Cup on their way to the final?

7. The winning Spurs goal away to West Ham United on 24 November 2001 came from a player who moved to Upton Park later in his career. Who was he?

8. The worst 45 minutes of the season was undoubtedly the collapse after leading Manchester United at half time by 3-0 at White Hart Lane on 29 September 2001. However, perhaps the most disappointing 90 minutes was the 4-0 home defeat in the FA Cup sixth round by Chelsea. Two of their scorers that day later joined Spurs. Who were they?

9. The media called Blackburn Rovers the 'underdogs' in the League Cup Final against Spurs, but there was only one league place between them, and Rovers won the game 2-1. The Spurs team contained an ex-Blackburn player, and the Blackburn team contained someone who would later play for Spurs. Who were the two players?

10. Which club did Les Ferdinand score a hat-trick against in a League Cup tie at White Hart Lane?

QUIZ No. 76

TOTTENHAM HOTSPUR – SEASON 2002/03

1. Did Spurs finish in the top half or bottom half of the Premier League in 2002/03?

2. On 11 September 2002, Spurs were leading 2-1 at Craven Cottage against Fulham, when Fulham were awarded a penalty in the 84th minute, and, after scoring with it, went on to win the game in the last minute. The scorer from the spot kick later joined Spurs. Who was he?

3. Four days later, instead of a 3-2 defeat to a London club, they had a 3-2 win when West Ham United visited the Lane. The winning goal was another last-minute affair featuring a Spurs defender. Who scored their winner?

4. An early Christmas present was delivered to those fans who ventured north to Manchester City on 23 December as Spurs ran out winners by that same score line again. Simon Davies got one of them, and the other two were shared by players who also shared surnames beginning with a 'P'. Who were the two players?

5. At White Hart Lane on 29 January Spurs, were beaten by a 90th-minute goal at home to Newcastle United. The culprit later joined Spurs. Who was he?

6. Something similar happened when Spurs went down 2-0 at Upton Park on 1 March. One of the scorers had recently left Spurs and the other would soon be joining them. Which two players got the goals?

7. The two domestic cup competitions were disappointing, Spurs managing to beat just one club. That was on 1 October 2002, in the League Cup, when which team departed down the M4 after losing 1-0 to a Teddy Sheringham goal?

8. Which goalkeeper didn't miss a game in the Premier League for Spurs in the 2002/03 season?

9. Which midfielder who started over 30 league games was voted the club's 'Player of the Year'?

10. Who was Spurs' leading goalscorer in the Premier League, his 13 goals being just enough to beat Teddy Sheringham on 12?

QUIZ No. 77

TOTTENHAM HOTSPUR –
SEASON 2003/04

1. A tough season that ended with Spurs in 14th place in the Premier League. Which manager was sacked in September after a 3-1 home defeat by Southampton, and who replaced him on a caretaker basis?

2. He played just one season for the club, starting 12 games, and coming on as a substitute a further ten times. Two of his three league goals came in a 4-1 home win over Birmingham City on 7 January 2004. Who was he?

3. Who scored his first Spurs goal in a 2-1 home win over Liverpool on 17 January 2004?

4. Spurs were involved in a 4-4 home draw with Leicester City on 22 February 2004. One of the visitor's goals was an own goal from a Spurs player, two more came from players who also played for Spurs in their careers, and the other came from a man who shares a surname with a Spurs player of this decade. How many of Leicester's goalscorers can you name?

5. A Freddie Kanoute hat-trick deposited which London club out of the FA Cup when Spurs won a third-round tie 3-0 at White Hart Lane on 3 January 2004?

6. Which club did Spurs meet in both domestic cups, beating them in the League Cup, before becoming a laughing stock by losing 4-3 against ten men in an FA Cup replay at White Hart Lane, after leading 3-0 at the interval?

7. After a 3-0 League Cup win at Coventry, Spurs put West Ham United out after extra time in the next round at White Hart Lane. Which Spurs forward, who later played for West Ham, scored the only goal of the game?

8. Spurs eventually lost on penalties in the fifth round of the League Cup to the team that went on to win it. Who were they?

9. Which colour scored for Spurs in the Premier League that season?

10. The season can be neatly summed up for suffering Spurs fans. Of the five London clubs in the Premier League in 2003/04, Arsenal won the title, Chelsea were second, and the other two teams, not known for finishing above Spurs very often, both did so this time. Who were they?

QUIZ No. 78

TOTTENHAM HOTSPUR – SEASON 2004/05

1. Which manager parted company with the club for personal reasons 12 games into the new season?

2. The plaudits for being top league goalscorer, top FA Cup goalscorer and top League Cup goalscorer all went to the same player. Who?

3. Spurs won 1-0 away at Newcastle United and Everton in the first half of the Premier League season. The winning goals were scored by two players for whom those goals were their first and last league goals for the club. Which two men scored them?

4. In the League Cup, an away draw in Lancashire held few fears for Spurs as they won 6-0, 4-3, and 3-0 in that county in the first three rounds. Which three teams bit the dust?

5. When they finally got the home tie they wanted it did for them after extra time and a penalty shoot-out against which club?

6. Spurs looked promising in the FA Cup too, beating Brighton & Hove Albion, West Bromwich Albion and Nottingham Forest before being eliminated 1-0 away to which club in the quarter-final?

7. On 16 March 2005, Spurs lost 2-0 to Charlton Athletic at the Valley. One of their goalscorers later joined Spurs. Who was he?

8. Exactly one month later, on 16 April, who scored a wonder goal at the Kop end at Anfield in a 2-2 draw with Liverpool?

9. Spurs fans had already seen a Ziege and a Zamora at White Hart Lane, but on the first day of 2005 another 'Z' was on the score sheet for Spurs when they beat Everton 5-2. Who was he?

10. Which young Irish defender did more than just contain the opposition when he scored against both clubs from the second city? Firstly, on 2 April, he got the Spurs goal in a 1-1 away draw with Birmingham City, and repeated the dose when Aston Villa were beaten 5-1 at Tottenham on 1 May 2005.

QUIZ No. 79

TOTTENHAM HOTSPUR –
SEASON 2005/06

1. A strange season. The big positive was the club finishing fifth, their best league position since coming third in which pre-Premier League season?

2. However, the circumstances in which they finished in that position were frustrating to say the least. A win on the last day of the season would have brought a Champions League place with it for the following season. Who beat them 2-1?

3. The night before the game the players had stayed at a hotel and had felt ill after their meal, prompting rumours of deliberate food poisoning. It turned out to probably be something else, but what was the whole affair called?

4. Another frustrating aspect of the season was the way Spurs capitulated at the first hurdle in both domestic cup competitions to clubs from a lower division. In the third round of the FA Cup they held a 2-0 lead away from home before contriving to lose 3-2 to which Midlands club?

5. In the League Cup it was even worse when they managed to get beaten by a club from the fourth tier of English football. Which club turned them over 1-0?

6. Who was the only Spurs player to appear in all 38 league matches for the club?

7. A Spurs player was sent off against Chelsea at White Hart Lane in August 2005, and another performed the same feat at Anfield against Liverpool in January 2006. Who were the two offenders?

8. Michael Dawson outdid both of them in the red card stakes, managing to get sent off on a London ground in January, and one much further north in April. On which two grounds?

9. On New Year's Eve, Spurs beat Newcastle United 2-0 at White Hart Lane. Which player, who only went on to score two more, scored his first goal for the club in that game?

10. When Spurs won 3-2 at Charlton Athletic on 1 October 2005, one of the home side's players scored both their goals before later joining Spurs. Who was he?

QUIZ No. 80

TOTTENHAM HOTSPUR – SEASON 2006/07

1. Spurs matched their fifth-place finish of the previous season despite long-term injuries to players. Who, with 12, scored the most league goals for the club?

2. Goalkeeper Paul Robinson had a game to remember on 17 March 2007, when he scored with a free kick from his own half in a 3-1 win at White Hart Lane. Wikipedia called it a lob. It's certainly the strangest lob I've ever seen! Which club conceded the goal?

3. Not only did he get on the scoring sheet, but Paul Robinson also didn't miss a single league game all season. Which Spurs defender ran him closest by missing just one?

4. The season's most exciting league encounter came at Upton Park on 4 March 2007 when Spurs rallied from 3-2 down to equalise through Berbatov in the 89th minute, before winning it at the death with a goal from which player?

5. Although it was a source of great irritation to lose an FA Cup replay at home to Chelsea, especially after holding a 3-1 lead at Stamford Bridge in the first match, Spurs did pull off that rare beast of the time in the shape of a home league win over their West London rivals, beating them 2-1 on Bonfire night. Who banged in the winner?

6. Which seaside town did Spurs get drawn against in both the FA Cup and the League Cup?

7. In their opening League Cup tie Spurs won 5-0 away at a club in the fourth tier of English football. They were a club that nearly a decade later would see Spurs poach an excellent young player. Who were the club and the player?

8. Port Vale gave Spurs a fright in the next round when they led at White Hart Lane going into the last ten minutes. Which Spurs midfielder grabbed the equaliser and then put them in front in extra time on their way to a 3-1 win?

9. Two days before Christmas, Spurs lost 3-1 at Newcastle. Spurs' goal was scored by a midfielder, as was one of the home side's as well. The two players had both earlier played for the same club, and the Newcastle man eventually wound up at Spurs. Who were the two players?

10. Who scored his only league goal for Spurs in a 2-1 win at Manchester City in December 2006 after signing from Coventry City?

QUIZ No. 81

TOTTENHAM HOTSPUR – SEASON 2007/08

1. The highlight of the season was the arrival of the first trophy at White Hart Lane for nine years, and winning the League Cup was given an extra gloss by the fact that it was the Chelsea fans who left Wembley in a depressed state. Whose penalty got Spurs back in the game?

2. Another pleasure for Spurs fans came with the fact that Arsenal were demolished 5-1 in the second leg of the semi-final after a 1-1 draw in the first leg. Which Arsenal player scored an own goal in that second leg?

3. Who was the only Spurs player to score against two different clubs on the way to the final?

4. Which newly signed centre-forward got his first league goal for Spurs in a 4-0 win over Derby County on 18 August 2007 at White Hart Lane?

5. On the first day of the following month, in an exciting 3-3 draw against Fulham at Craven Cottage, which new signing from Southampton got off the mark for his new club?

6. Someone else scored his first Spurs goal in that game, and exactly one month later on 1 October got a vital 93rd-minute equaliser in a 4-4 draw with Aston Villa at White Hart Lane. Who was he?

7. How many goals did Dimitar Berbatov score in a league game against Reading at White Hart Lane on 29 December 2007?

8. Spurs got a 2-2 draw at Anfield on 7 October 2007, when which player scored for them in the last minute of the first half and the first minute of the second half?

9. Which popular Spurs manager was sacked during the first half of the season, and who replaced him?

10. March 2008 brought debut goals for two more Spurs players. On the 9th, Gilberto scored one of the goals in a 4-0 White Hart Lane win over another London club, while on the 22nd Jamie O'Hara scored in a 2-0 home win against another Premier League club situated somewhat south of Tottenham. Who were the two defeated clubs?

QUIZ No. 82

TOTTENHAM HOTSPUR –
SEASON 2008/09

1. Spurs eventually finished eighth, but that didn't look likely after the first eight games of 2008/09. How many of the 24 points on offer did Spurs reel in?

2. Which manager was appointed to deal with the crisis, and which club did he leave to join Spurs?

3. The one thing that did get sorted was the Spurs defence at White Hart Lane. They set a new club record for home goals conceded in a season and had the best record in the Premier League. How many goals did they let in over their 19 home league games, and which goalkeeper played in the vast majority of them?

4. Who scored in every League Cup match leading up to the final, was unsurprisingly Spurs top scorer in the competition, and also scored the most FA Cup goals into the bargain?

5. In July, Teemu Tainio, Pascal Chimbonda and Steed Malbranque all left Spurs to join the same club. Which one?

6. Which expensive new signing scored his first league goal for Spurs when they lost 2-1 away to Newcastle United on 21 December 2008?

7. As is widely known, Manchester United beat Spurs on penalties after a 0-0 draw after extra time in the League Cup Final of 2009. But which club knocked Spurs out of the FA Cup?

8. Which Spurs player scored three goals for them in four days in November, but didn't score for them outside those four days? He got two in a 4-2 win over Liverpool at White Hart Lane on 12 November in the League Cup, and four days later got their goal in a 2-1 defeat at Fulham.

9. After great service to the club, one Spurs player left in the close season to join Blackburn Rovers, while another player came in the opposite direction and made an instant impact at the Emirates. Who were the two players?

10. In the League Cup semi-final over two legs, Spurs took a handsome 4-1 lead into the second leg. However, they made heavy weather of getting over the line, losing the second leg 3-0 over the 90 minutes, the match going into extra time before Spurs prevailed 6-4 on aggregate. Who were the club that gave them the fright?

QUIZ No. 83

TOTTENHAM HOTSPUR –
SEASON 2009/10

1. An excellent season that culminated in an exciting game away to Manchester City in May that Spurs had to win to deny City a Champions League place and grab it themselves. It looked like the odds were against it, but whose vital goal made it happen on a great night?

2. In what season had Spurs last qualified for the competition?

3. Tottenham's leading goalscorer in both the Premier League and the FA Cup also appeared on the pitch more times than any other player, with 31 starts and three off the bench. Who was he?

4. In the close season, Spurs signed two players with the same first name from the same club, namely Sheffield United. As is sometimes customary now, they immediately loaned one of them back to the Yorkshire club, although of the two he eventually made the bigger impact. Who were the two players?

5. Two Spurs defenders made a great start to the season by scoring the goals by which they beat Liverpool on the opening day at White Hart Lane. One was a left-sided player who had been at the club a while, and the other was a central defender making his league debut. Who were the two players?

6. Who weighed in with four goals when Spurs beat Burnley 5-0 on 26 September 2009?

7. When Spurs drew a league fixture 2-2 at Bolton on 3 October 2009, their goals were scored by two players scoring in the league for them for the first time. One was a midfielder who came from Portsmouth, while the other was a right-sided defender who arrived from Manchester City. Who were they?

8. Fourth place in the league was supplemented by a fine FA Cup run, albeit one that ended in semi-final defeat against underdogs Portsmouth. After accounting for Peterborough, Spurs were taken to a replay each time before beating three clubs who shared their colours. Who were they?

9. In the League Cup, Spurs beat Everton at home before going out at Old Trafford. Earlier, away to two clubs from the division below them, Spurs had won both games 5-1. Who did they beat?

10. On 22 November 2009 Spurs beat Wigan 9-1 at White Hart Lane. Since the Premier League began, only two other clubs have scored nine times in a game, one before that game and one after. Who are the two teams, and which two clubs were on the receiving end?

QUIZ No. 84

TOTTENHAM HOTSPUR – SEASON 2010/11

1. Spurs finished fifth, being beaten just once at home in 19 games. The club that inflicted the defeat must have enjoyed it slightly more than usual. Who were they and why might they have been extra pleased with their 1-0 away win?

2. Which Spurs midfielder, with 32, made the most league starts for them in 2010/11?

3. On 28 November Spurs beat Liverpool 2-1 at White Hart Lane. Which Liverpool defender scored at both ends in the game?

4. Which adventurous Spurs full-back scored Premier League goals in a 3-1 win at home to Wolves, and in a 4-2 defeat at Bolton?

5. Rafael Van der Vaart came to the club from Real Madrid in the close season and proved to be a big hit with the fans. Which club did Spurs beat 2-1 home and away in the league, to which his contribution was all four goals?

6. Which Spurs winger scored against Newcastle United in a 2-0 win at White Hart Lane in December, and then in the following month got a last-minute equaliser against the same club away from home?

7. In the two domestic cup competitions Spurs met three London clubs and no others. In the FA Cup they won 3-0 against a team from the south east of the capital, before going out 4-0 at the hands of one from the south west. In the League Cup they went out after extra time at home to someone you want to lose to as little as possible! Who were the three London clubs they encountered in the two cup competitions?

8. Which Spurs player scored twice at home to Stoke City on 9 April, and in both the home and away matches against Blackburn Rovers?

9. Which Brazilian midfielder scored his first goal for Spurs in a 2-1 defeat at Stamford Bridge on 30 April 2011?

10. In November it looked like business as usual when Spurs went 2-0 down at The Emirates. But a stunning second-half fight back ended up sending the Spurs fans home in a very joyful mood. Who headed the winner when they left The Emirates 3-2 to the good?

QUIZ No. 85

TOTTENHAM HOTSPUR –
SEASON 2011/12

1. Spurs enjoyed a relatively successful season, but their fourth-place finish was not rewarded with a Champions League place. Why?

2. Spurs had only themselves to blame as they ceded third place to Arsenal of all teams on the final day of the season when West Brom's goalkeeper presented the Gunners with three goals! At its best, how many points did Spurs lead Arsenal by during the season?

3. An ex-Arsenal player became top league goalscorer for Spurs with 17. Who was he and from which club did Spurs buy him?

4. Spurs had a fine FA Cup run until they ran out of steam annoyingly in the semi-final against Chelsea. In the fourth and fifth rounds they beat two teams from Hertfordshire, the second after a replay. Who were they?

5. In their first FA Cup tie of the season they beat Cheltenham 3-0 at White Hart Lane. Which signing from Barcelona scored his first and only goal in that competition for Spurs?

6. The real drama of the tournament came at White Hart Lane on 1 7 March 2012 with the visit of Bolton Wanderers for the sixth-round tie. A Bolton player suffered a cardiac arrest just before half time and the match was abandoned with the score at 1-1. Who was the unfortunate Bolton player, which referee abandoned the game, and who scored the Spurs goal?

7. Ten days later when the match was restaged, Spurs won 3-1, their opening goal coming from a tough centre-half they had acquired from Blackburn Rovers. Who was he?

8. Which Spurs player, between 24 September and 30 October 2011, scored in five consecutive league games for Spurs against Wigan, Arsenal, Newcastle United, Blackburn Rovers and QPR?

9. Spurs' progress in the League Cup was non-existent. Their opening game produced a 0-0 away draw but they were eased out 7-6 on penalties by which club?

10. Spurs' progress in the league was reflected in three of their players being chosen for the PFA 'Team of the Year'. One was a defender, another was a defensive midfielder, while the third was an exciting wide left man. Who were they?

QUIZ No. 86

TOTTENHAM HOTSPUR – SEASON 2012/13

1. Harry Redknapp and Spurs parted company in the close season, paving the way for which highly touted young manager to take over?

2. Another to leave was Luka Modric, in August 2012. Which club did he join and how much did Spurs get in return?

3. The new boss had his first win when Spurs won 3-1 away on 16 September 2012 in the Premier League, and in doing so helped set a new attendance record of 24,106 for the ground they won on. Who did they beat?

4. In this season, Gareth Bale scored 21 league goals and became the first Spurs player to reach 20 in the Premier League this century. Who was the last Spurs player to score 20 goals in a Premier League season?

5. Spurs scored four times on only one ground during the season in the league. It came on Boxing Day, when, assisted by Bale's first Premier League hat-trick, they won 4-0, but on which ground?

6. Most players feared playing the Manchester United of this era, but one Spurs newcomer didn't. On 29 September 2012, he scored his first Spurs goal in their first Old Trafford win since 1989. Then, in the last minute of the return game at White Hart Lane on 20 January 2013, with the snow swirling round the ground, he got the equaliser for the home side. Who are we talking about?

7. Bale scored two on a few occasions during the season, but the two he managed on 28 November 2012 were a bit different in that he scored at both ends when Spurs won 2-1 at home to which club?

8. In the FA Cup, Spurs went out to Leeds United in the fourth round, and, in the League Cup, Norwich City did for them by the same 2-1 score line. Previously in these competitions they had won 3-0 against two teams beginning with a 'C'. Who were they?

9. On 17 March Spurs lost 1-0 at home to another London club in a result that proved costly at the season's end. Which club beat them, which ex-Spurs manager brought them to White Hart Lane, and which ex-Spur scored their winning goal?

10. It was costly because a late Arsenal run denied Spurs a Champions League spot. When Spurs had beaten them 2-1 at home on 3 March they created a club record of Premier League games undefeated. How many?

QUIZ No. 87

TOTTENHAM HOTSPUR – SEASON 2013/14

1. With the sale of Gareth Bale to Real Madrid, Spurs spread the cash widely in the transfer market, buying a number of players. Before October was out, one of the newcomers had got the winning goal from the penalty spot three times in 1-0 wins over Crystal Palace, Swansea City and Hull City, the first of those on his Premier League debut at Selhurst Park. Who was he?

2. On 4 December 2013, which two Spurs players, one a defender and one a midfielder, both scored their first Premier League goals for the club in a 2-1 win at Craven Cottage against Fulham?

3. Manager Villas-Boas got the sack a week before Santa needed his after two heavy defeats. Who took over the reins on an 18-month contract that wasn't honoured because he was 'too outspoken', a crime no other manager has ever been remotely guilty of?

4. It was galling that Spurs lost to London clubs in both domestic cups, but the same two sides also did the double over Spurs in the league. Not nice! Who were they?

5. On 19 February 2014, Spurs won 3-1 at Swansea to complete a run of five successive away wins in the top flight for the first time since which season?

6. Which midfielder, signed from Dutch club Twente, scored the final goal in a 4-0 League Cup win away to Aston Villa on the night of 24 September 2013?

7. Which Brazilian player got a late winner for Spurs away to Cardiff City on 22 September 2013?

8. It was a season in which a few Spurs players were no stranger to the red card, including the answer to the previous question. To be fair, some of them were rescinded, but which Spurs player got himself sent off at two London grounds, Stamford Bridge and Upton Park?

9. Among the good things that the man in charge did in the five months he was given was to get a tune out of Adebayor and introduce Harry Kane to the first team. The latter promptly repaid the manager's trust in him by scoring in his first three outings, his debut celebrated with a 5-1 win over which club at White Hart Lane?

10. On 23 March 2014, Spurs found themselves 2-0 down at home to Southampton, but rallied with the help of two Eriksen goals before whose strike won the game for Spurs in injury time?

QUIZ No. 88

TOTTENHAM HOTSPUR – SEASON 2014/15

1. Mauricio Pochettino was the new man tasked with the job of taking Tottenham forward. Which country did he hail from and from which club did Spurs prise him?

2. Although by finishing fifth Spurs didn't reach the promised land of the Champions League, the season was notable for the pace at which Harry Kane stripped all expectations of his abilities. He scored 31 goals in all competitions. You had to go back to the previous century to find when this was last done at Spurs – by which player?

3. Only one man in the top flight scored more, with 32. Who was that?

4. Spurs' most creative player was also the only man to be on the pitch in every one of their 38 league games. Who was he?

5. During the season, in away matches against Hull City and QPR, and a home game against Swansea City, three ex-Spurs players scored against them. Who were they?

6. New Year's Day brought the most memorable game of the season when Spurs beat Chelsea 5-3 at a white-hot Lane! One of the five came from the penalty spot. Who took it?

7. Among Spurs players fielding red cards were Fazio and Chiriches, but which man was sent off on the first day at Upton Park, and again at home to Stoke City on 9 November?

8. After a replay win over Burnley, Spurs went out of the FA Cup to Leicester City, but in the League Cup it was a different story as they went all the way to the final itself, only to be denied by Chelsea at Wembley. Which Spurs player was unfortunate enough to concede an own goal in that final?

9. In their first League Cup tie that season Spurs beat Nottingham Forest 3-1 and one of their goals was scored by a young prospect whose career was cut short a couple of years later by a freak injury while playing for another club. Who was he?

10. Harry Kane was called up to the England squad in the same week that he scored his first Premier League hat-trick on 21 March 2015 at White Hart Lane in a 4-3 win over which club?

QUIZ No. 89

TOTTENHAM HOTSPUR – SEASON 2015/16

1. Although the season's end brought typical Tottenham frustration in yet again conceding league bragging rights to Arsenal, the Champions League target was achieved by the third-place finish. Spurs lost the same number of games at home as they did away. What did the home and away defeats add up to?

2. After a slow start, Harry Kane enjoyed a great season, winning the 'Golden Boot' with 25 league goals. Who was the only other Spurs player to reach double figures?

3. It helped that Kane started every league game. This record was matched by just one other Spurs player whose role was at the other end of the pitch. Who was it?

4. Who scored his first goal for Spurs at home to Watford on 6 February 2016, his strike proving to be the winner in a 1-0 score line?

5. Arguably the most exciting game brought a 2-1 win at Manchester City in a key match on 14 February 2016. Eriksen slid in the Spurs winner in the 83rd minute and the Spurs fans behind that goal made it a moment to remember. Why was Eriksen likely to have been more happy than usual with his winning goal?

6. On 3 January 2016, Spurs drew 1-1 at Everton, where the home side's goal was scored by a former Spurs player. Who was he?

7. We will draw a veil over the League Cup defeat by another club from North London, but it was also very disheartening to be knocked out of the FA Cup in the fifth round by another London club who won 1-0 at White Hart Lane. Who were they?

8. Previous to that, Spurs had beaten Leicester after a replay, and won 4-1 at Colchester, where Chadli bagged two and Carroll also scored. The other two scorers were both Tottenham men with surnames starting with a 'D'. One of them scored the other Spurs goal while the other put through his own goal for Colchester's best moment of the game. Who were the two players?

9. For the first time, Spurs had four representatives in the PFA 'Team of the Year'. Kane, Alli, and Alderweireld were all included. Who was the fourth player?

10. Spurs scored five times just once in the season away from home on 25 October. Who did they beat with the aid of some charitable goalkeeping, and which player scored a hat-trick?

QUIZ No. 90

TOTTENHAM HOTSPUR – SEASON 2016/17

1. Although Chelsea winning the league was never going to be good news for Spurs fans, Tottenham's second-place finish guaranteed Champions League football again and was the club's highest finishing position since which season?

2. In what was sadly the club's last season at White Hart Lane, they pulled out all the stops to remain undefeated there. Who were the only two clubs in the 19 matches to take a point away with them?

3. A top-flight club record came with the number of home games won in succession. What was that figure?

4. Three ex-Spurs players scored against the club in the Premier league, the first in a 1-1 draw at West Brom in October, the second a last-minute consolation for Watford when they lost 4-1 at home to Spurs in January, and the third gave Swansea the lead over Spurs at the Liberty Stadium in April, a lead they held until Spurs found the net three times in five minutes at the death. Who were the three former Spurs players?

5. After removing Aston Villa from the FA Cup in the third round, Spurs had a large fright in the fourth round at White Hart Lane. Trailing 3-2 to fourth-tier opponents in the last minute of normal time, an Alli goal drew them level before Son won it deep into added-on time. The Spurs crowd applauded the visitors from the pitch. Who were they?

6. After that let off, Spurs met two London clubs, winning 3-0 away and 6-0 at home with the help of hat-tricks from Kane and Son. Unfortunately, another London club beat Spurs in the semi-final, but we won't go there! Which two clubs did they beat?

7. At least the dear old place saw a hatful of cup goals in its final season, 17 to be precise. The FA Cup has been covered, but which side from Skybet League One did they overpower 5-0 in their first League Cup game?

8. That game was played on 21 September 2016, and a local lad scored his first goal for Spurs in it. Who was he?

9. No Spurs player was on the pitch for all 38 Premier League games, but who came closest with 37?

10. Finally, Harry Kane deserves congratulations for winning the 'Golden Boot' again with 29 goals. His total was boosted by hat-tricks in January and February in 4-0 home wins over which two Midlands clubs?

QUIZ No. 91

TOTTENHAM HOTSPUR – SEASON 2017/18

1. Spurs finished third, and in the process became London's top club for the first time since finishing seventh above, in order, QPR, Wimbledon, Chelsea, Arsenal, West Ham United and a relegated Crystal Palace. In which season?

2. Chelsea may typically have ruined Spurs' first Premier League game at Wembley, but they were made to look the fools at last on 1 April 2018, when Spurs broke their Stamford Bridge hoodoo by winning there for the first time since 1990. A superb goal by Dele Alli helped them win by what score?

3. Which powerful midfielder got his first league goal for Spurs in a 4-0 win at Huddersfield on 30 September 2017?

4. Firstly, in October, with a figure of 80,827, and then again in January with 81,978, Spurs set new Premier League attendance records in home games against which two clubs at Wembley?

5. Which goalkeeper performed well on his debut at Wembley in a 1-0 win over Crystal Palace on Firework night?

6. We will gloss over the League Cup, but Spurs reached the FA Cup semi-final, only to lose for an incredible eighth time in a row at that stage of the competition, this time to Manchester United. On their way to the semi-final, they knocked out which two Welsh clubs?

7. Rochdale gave Spurs a scare in the fifth round when Spurs were held 2-2 at Spotland, before a 6-1 replay win. Which Spurs player who scored in the first game would have had memories of that ground and what would those memories have consisted of?

8. Which defender scored his first goal for Spurs on 13 December 2017, in a 2-0 home win over Brighton?

9. During the season Harry Kane equalled one record and broke another. Firstly, a December hat-trick in a 3-0 win at Burnley meant he had scored 36 Premier League goals in a calendar year to equal a record. Secondly, his two goals in a 4-0 home win over Everton in January meant that, with a total of 97 Premier League goals, he had broken the Spurs club record. Which two players held these records?

10. Which Spurs player scored his first goal for the club on his debut against the team he had joined them from in a 2-0 away win in Wales on 2 January 2018?

QUIZ No. 92

TOTTENHAM HOTSPUR - SEASON 2018/19

1. The season was notable for Spurs' European exploits that so nearly brought home the big prize, which would have rendered Champions League qualification redundant. What was unique about their away record in the Premier League?

2. What was unusual about Harry Kane's goal in a 3-1 home win over Fulham on 18 August?

3. Which Spurs player endured a tough baptism when he gave away two penalties on his debut at Molineux, before turning things around a week later by scoring the winner against Crystal Palace at Selhurst Park on 10 November?

4. Two players whose surnames start with a 'W' scored one goal each during the season. The first man got a last-minute winner away to Fulham, while the second put the cherry on the cake after a Lucas Moura hat-trick in a 4-0 home win over Huddersfield. Who were the two players?

5. Whose penalty did Hugo Lloris save to preserve the 1-1 score line near the end of the match against Arsenal on 2 March 2019?

6. Which two London clubs knocked Spurs out of the two domestic cup competitions, the FA Cup defeat coming in the fourth round, while the League Cup defeat was more painful coming as it did in the semi-final on penalties?

7. In that latter competition Spurs had knocked out two other London clubs to reach that semi-final stage. Which two?

8. The only FA Cup tie Spurs won was something of a breeze when they scored seven without reply away from home. Llorente scored a hat-trick and a Spurs defender had the rare distinction of scoring twice. Who did Spurs beat 7-0 and which defender contributed the two goals?

9. Although Spurs eventually went out of the League Cup on penalties, they were actually fortunate to win by this method in the first game of the tournament after a 2-2 home draw with which club?

10. On which league club's ground did Spurs have both Son and Foyth sent off on 4 May 2019?

QUIZ No. 93

TOTTENHAM HOTSPUR – SEASON 2019/20

1. It was an eventful season, but extremely uneventful in April and May when there was no football for reasons the whole world knows about. The big news before Christmas came on 19 November when which well-liked Spurs manager was sacked?

2. Spurs had made a poor start to their league programme, but had also been knocked out of the League Cup on penalties after a 0-0 draw away to which club from the fourth tier of English football?

3. Penalties were their undoing in the FA Cup as well, when after wins over Middlesbrough and Southampton that both required replays, they exited the competition on penalties after a 1-1 home draw after extra time against which club?

4. In the FA Cup third-round replay win against Middlesbrough on 14 January 2020, Spurs' goals were scored by two players with surnames beginning with the same letter. Who were they?

5. Jose Mourinho took over at Spurs the day after the previous manager's sacking and promptly won his first game in charge by 3-2 away from home. Who did Spurs beat?

6. Those lucky enough to be at the Tottenham Hotspur Stadium on 7 December 2019 were treated to one of those goals that comes along very rarely indeed, when Son ran through the opposition from the edge of his own box. Which club's players were left scratching their heads after going down 5-0?

7. A week or so later, Spurs won 3-2 at Aston Villa. Which Spurs player netted for both sides in the game?

8. Covid-19 sounds like it could be an international football team, but had the effect of bringing football and most other things to a halt in mid-March. It was 19 June in this crazy season when Spurs next played, drawing 1-1 at home with which club in an empty stadium where the well-advertised ability to pour a million pints of beer in two minutes flat was suddenly redundant?

9. The delights of VAR had brought the death of spontaneity to the game and ensured that those who had paid to watch the game were the last to know what was going on. Spurs suffered badly from this nonsense in two away games at the end of the season when Kane had a goal disallowed and a clear penalty turned down. On which two grounds did these injustices occur?

10. Spurs looked a better organised team after the enforced break and clinched a Europa League place after winning how many of their remaining nine games?

QUIZ No. 94

THE TOTTENHAM HOTSPUR STADIUM

1. Plans to move to a new stadium were in the offing as early as 2007, but the Northumberland Development Project, as it was known, finally came to fruition after a resubmitted plan was accepted by Haringey Council and ratified by London's Lord Mayor in 2010. Who was he?

2. After several appeals the Compulsory Purchase orders required were finally confirmed by the Secretary of State for Communities and Local Government. That politician is often found in a glass jar on a pub bar and also once discovered the World Cup under a bush. Who was he?

3. For a variety of reasons, the ground's capacity is never actually recorded by a match-day attendance. Is that figure 62,303, 62,404, 62,505 or 62,606?

4. The South Stand is the designated home end and efforts have been made to produce a wall of sound similar to the 'Yellow Wall' design at one end of the Signal Iduna Park Stadium. Which German club plays there?

5. The magnificent cockerel that used to look out across London from White Hart Lane has been replaced by a much larger replica that has been erected on the roof of the South Stand. Why has it got dents in it?

6. After a few false starts and an under-18s game against Southampton on 24 March 2019, the new ground was officially opened with an exhibition match involving which Italian club?

7. Spurs eventually played their long-awaited first league game at the new stadium on 3 April 2019. Who were their first visitors?

8. Who scored Spurs' first goal in the new ground in that match?

9. Someone had to score the first goal against Spurs in their new ground, and it came on 27 April 2019. Who scored the goal and which London club was he playing for?

10. If I were an American Football fan I would not be overpleased to be asked to pay a four-figure sum to travel half way round the world to watch my local team. But that is the madness we now inhabit! For how long is Tottenham's deal to put on American Football at their ground?

QUIZ No. 95

'TOTTENHAM TEARAWAYS' – SENDINGS OFF

1. Which Spurs player was sent off away to Olympique Leonnais of France in the first leg of the second round of the European Cup Winners' Cup on 29 November 1967?

2. Spurs have had a number of their players sent off while playing for England under-21s, but only one managed to repeat the offence in 2008 after the first occasion the previous year. Who was he?

3. Which Spurs player, after some provocation from Robbie Savage, was sent off in the 1999 League Cup Final at Wembley when Spurs beat Leicester City 1-0?

4. The first Spurs player to be sent off in a game against Arsenal received his marching orders on 27 December 1976, in a 2-2 draw at White Hart Lane. Who was he?

5. In this century two Dutch internationals have been sent off playing for Spurs against Arsenal. The first came at Highbury in a 1-1 draw in 2006, while the second came in a 4-2 defeat at The Emirates in 2018. Who are the two Spurs players?

6. Which unlikely Spurs player was sent off three times in 2019, and whose nine-year record set at Wigan Athletic and Sunderland did he equal?

7. Which Spurs defender was sent off on his league debut for the club away to West Ham United in September 2017?

8. On 25 February 2012, which Spurs player who was having a good game and had just put Spurs 2-0 ahead away from home at the Emirates, was sent off in a game-changing incident that ended up with Spurs losing 5-2?

9. Jan Vertonghen is the only Spurs player to be sent off in a Champions League game at Wembley. It happened in September 2017, against which German club?

10. Which Spurs player was sent off in the away leg of the Champions League quarter-final against Real Madrid on 5 April 2011?

QUIZ No. 96

TRUE OR FALSE - PART 1 - ANYTHING GOES

1. In doing the double in 1960/61 Aston Villa were the only club that Spurs beat three times. True or false?

2. Bolton Wanderers are the only side Spurs have been promoted to the top flight with more than once. True or false?

3. Sandy Brown is the only Spurs player to score four goals in an FA Cup semi-final. True or false?

4. Spurs have played in five European finals. On one of those five occasions they met a team that were defending the trophy as the previous year's winners. True or false?

5. Spurs are the only English club to have won a European trophy on two occasions in their own city. True or false?

6. West Ham United and Spurs are the only two English clubs to have won a European trophy more times than they have won their domestic league title. True or false?

7. Alan Mullery was the first post-war Spurs player to captain England. True or false?

8. Spurs have never played the same club in successive FA Cup semi-finals. True or false?

9. In the inter-war period, Spurs' highest finishing position in top-flight football was second place, which they achieved in 1921/22. True or false?

10. In the post-war era Burnley are the only club Spurs have played against in the FA Cup in three successive seasons. True or false?

QUIZ No. 97

TRUE OR FALSE - PART 2 - 'THE DOUBLE'

1. Manchester City were the first club to beat Spurs in the 1960/61 double season. True or false?

2. In that season, Spurs lost six times as many league games in 1961 as they did in 1960. True or false?

3. Spurs beat Arsenal 4-2 at home and 3-2 away in the double season. Les Allen was the only Spurs player to score in both games. True or false?

4. Until 1981/82 when the three points for a win system came in, Tottenham's total of 66 points was surpassed on just one occasion, when Liverpool got 68 points in 1978/79. True or false?

5. Spurs beat every other club in the league at least once in 1960/61. True or false?

6. In their 42 league matches, Spurs were involved in just one 0-0 draw, which came against Fulham at Craven Cottage. True or false?

7. Only Arsenal, with 127 goals in the league in 1930/31, have topped Spurs' total of 115 goals in the 1960/61 season. True or false?

8. John White scored 13 league goals, but failed to score in any of Spurs' FA Cup ties, despite playing in all seven games in the competition in which they scored 21 goals. True or false?

9. The gap between the largest and smallest attendance that watched Spurs in their double season of 49 league and cup matches was 78,343. True or false?

10. Manchester United were the only team to beat Spurs to nil in a league game that season. True or false?

QUIZ No. 98

VENUES

1. On which now defunct league ground did Spurs win the FA Cup for the first time after a replay against Sheffield United in 1901?

2. In which city did Spurs beat Atletico Madrid to win the European Cup Winners' Cup in 1963?

3. On which league ground did Spurs lose an FA Cup semi-final against Everton on 9 April 1995?

4. On which league ground did Spurs beat Wolves to win the FA Cup in 1921?

5. In which city did Spurs lose the 2019 Champions League Final to Liverpool?

6. On which now defunct league ground did Spurs beat Wolves 3-0 in an FA Cup semi-final replay in April 1981?

7. What is the only venue apart from Wembley that has hosted an Arsenal v Spurs FA Cup semi-final?

8. On which league ground did Spurs lose an FA Cup semi-final to Newcastle United on 11 April 1999?

9. Spurs played in their first FA Cup semi-final on 8 April 1901 when they beat West Bromwich Albion 4-0. Where was the game played?

10. Which league ground did Spurs first play a semi-final on in 1921 and last play one on in 1981?

QUIZ No. 99

WHAT'S IN A NAME?

All these Spurs players share their complete name with someone famous.
Who are they in each case?

1. Between 1899 and 1912 he played 339 times for Spurs and shares
   his name with a famous golfing father and son who won eight of the
   first 12 Opens between them.

2. Between 1935 and 1939 he played 51 times for Spurs, scoring 16
   goals before a move to Swansea Town. He shares his name with a
   well-known producer of hit records in the 1960s, 'Telstar' by the
   Tornados among them.

3. He came from Sheffield Wednesday in 1898 and left for Preston
   North End in 1901 after 40 Spurs appearances. He shares his name
   with a clever Liverpool and England schemer who, as a manager, led
   Brighton out at Wembley in the 1983 FA Cup Final.

4. He played for Spurs between 1925 and 1927 before leaving for
   Forest. He shares his name with an American singer who had hits in
   the 1960s with 'Sheila' and 'Dizzy'.

5. He came from Mansfield Town in 1932 and left for QPR in 1933.
   He shares his name with a Welsh footballer who has been capped
   over 50 times for his country while with Swansea, Liverpool and
   Stoke City.

6. He played 27 times for Spurs between 1987 and 1989 before leaving
   for Brentford where he clocked up over 160 appearances. He shares
   his name with a great fast bowler who often worked in tandem with
   Fred Trueman for England.

7. He played 29 times for Spurs between 1972 and 1974 before trying
   his luck with New York Cosmos. He shares his name with the
   Marshal played by James Arness in the TV series *Gunsmoke*, or, if
   you're old enough, the earlier and better *Gun Law*.

8. He played 38 matches for Spurs after signing from West Ham United in 1946. He shares his name with a famous heavyweight boxer who has the means to grill his opponents!

9. He played just over 100 games for Spurs between 1968 and 1973. He shares a name with the British racing driver who won our Grand Prix in 1958 but was tragically killed later that year in the German Grand Prix.

10. He played 264 games in goal for Spurs between 1959 and 1966 and shares his name with the man who composed the music for the CBS series *CSI: NY*.

QUIZ No. 100

WHITE HART LANE

1. On which ground were Spurs playing before their move to White Hart Lane in the summer of 1899?

2. The new ground was opened with a friendly against a club that prides itself as being the country's oldest league club. Who were they?

3. What was the official address of the new ground?

4. 34 years after becoming a club ground, White Hart Lane, in 1933, was finally honoured with an international fixture. Three more followed in 1935, 1937 and 1949. England won all four games they played on the ground, against France, Germany, Czechoslovakia and Italy. The most exciting was the match against the Czechs. What was the score?

5. What links the 1919/20, 1932/33, 1964/65 and 2016/17 seasons at White Hart Lane?

6. Who were the opposition when the White Hart Lane attendance record was set at 75,038 in a sixth-round FA Cup tie on 5 March 1938?

7. Although not favoured anything like as much as the likes of Villa Park, Hillsborough or Maine Road, White Hart Lane was used for FA Cup semi-finals. In fact, in 1950, in the space of four days, two London rivals did battle there in an FA Cup semi-final and the required replay. Who were they?

8. A semi-final record that the club could have done without, although it was through no fault of theirs, came in 1988 when the crowd of 25,963 for the FA Cup semi-final was the lowest since the war. Which two teams contested the game on 9 April that year?

9. What is the link between Tom Smith and Harry Kane concerning White Hart Lane?

10. Although it would have been appropriate if a Spurs player had scored the last-ever goal at the ground, at least the man who got it was a great player, and his goal didn't make any difference to a day that ended with a Spurs win. Who was he?

ANSWERS

QUIZ No. 1 ACROSS THE CAPITAL

1. Queens Park Rangers
2. Crystal Palace
3. Chelsea
4. Orient
5. Brentford
6. Fulham
7. Charlton Athletic
8. Millwall
9. Arsenal
10. West Ham United

QUIZ No. 2 ANYTHING GOES - PART 1

1. West Bromwich Albion and Coventry City
2. Henry (Ron and Thierry)
3. A bowl of lemons
4. Graeme Souness
5. Jones
6. The floodlights failed in the second half with Spurs losing 1-0. After a wait of around 20 minutes they came on again and Spurs scored four times in 15 minutes to win the game
7. Bert Trautmann broke his neck diving at Peter Murphy's feet
8. Ben Thatcher
9. The Inter-Toto Cup
10. Jimmy Greaves was playing for Spurs reserves before making his first-team debut

QUIZ No. 3 ANYTHING GOES - PART 2

1. Leicester City – 2-0
2. An England XI who they beat 3-2
3. The Texaco Cup
4. Bill Nicholson and Terry Neill, Christian Gross and George Graham, and Juande Ramos and Harry Redknapp
5. Michy Batshuayi own goal
6. Jan Vertonghen
7. Oldham
8. Newcastle United
9. Gary Lineker is the odd man out. The others have all scored for Spurs from the penalty spot in a Wembley final, whereas Lineker

missed from the spot against Forest in the 1991 cup final
10. They floated the club on the Stock Exchange

QUIZ No. 4 BIRTHPLACES

1. Morocco
2. Stepney
3. Dagenham
4. Nottingham and Southampton
5. Cheltenham
6. Sheffield
7. North-East
8. He was born in Murphy
9. Guernsey
10. Ladbroke Grove

QUIZ No. 5 THE CHELSEA CONNECTION

1. Les Allen and Bobby Smith
2. Jimmy Greaves
3. Micky Hazard
4. Terry Venables and George Graham
5. Gordon Durie
6. Andre Villas-Boas and Jose Mourinho
7. Graham Roberts
8. Danny Blanchflower
9. Glenn Hoddle
10. Gus Poyet

QUIZ No. 6 CHRISTMAS CRACKERS

1. Southampton and The Dell
2. Jimmy Cantrell
3. Sheffield Wednesday
4. Charlton Athletic
5. Les Bennett
6. Everton
7. Ipswich Town
8. West Bromwich Albion
9. Harry Kane
10. Everton 2 Spurs 6 and Spurs 5 Bournemouth 0

QUIZ No. 7 'COME ON YOU SPURS' (FANS)

1. Adele
2. Peter Ebdon
3. Sid Owen
4. Jeremy Noseda

5. Kenneth Branagh
6. Warren Mitchell
7. Peter Cook
8. Hunter Davies
9. A.J. Ayer
10. Barnaby Slater

QUIZ No. 8 CRYPTIC SCORERS AGAINST ARSENAL

1. Tim Sherwood
2. Chris Armstrong
3. Mitchell Thomas
4. Alan Brazil
5. John Duncan
6. Alfie Stokes
7. Martin Chivers
8. Garth Crooks
9. Ralph Coates
10. Micky Hazard

QUIZ No. 9 CRYPTIC SPURS

1. Derek Possee
2. Chris Waddle
3. Ricky Villa
4. Frank Saul
5. Jimmy Neighbour
6. Bert Middlemiss
7. Terry Dyson
8. Teddy Sheringham
9. Jimmy Pass
10. Mike England and Justin Edinburgh

QUIZ No. 10 DOUBLE DIAMONDS

1. Sheffield Wednesday
2. Ron Henry
3. Cliff Jones
4. Manchester City
5. Crewe Alexandra
6. Preston North End and Aston Villa
7. Terry Dyson
8. Arbroath
9. Smith and Jones
10. Birmingham

QUIZ No. 11 ENGLAND CRICKET CAPTAINS

1. Tom Atherton
2. John Brearley
3. Shaun Close
4. Billy Cook or Bobby Cook

5. Mark Gower
6. Alan Hutton
7. John Illingworth
8. Bobby Smith and six others
9. Paul Stewart
10. Arthur Willis

QUIZ No. 12 FA CUP FINALS – 1960s

1. Dave Mackay
2. Gordon Banks, Adam Blacklaw and Peter Bonetti
3. Bobby Smith
4. Joe Kinnear and Cyril Knowles
5. Frank McLintock
6. Cliff Jones
7. Pat Jennings and Alan Mullery
8. Tommy Baldwin, John Hollins, Pat Jennings and Jimmy Robertson
9. Norman
10. Terry Dyson with his head

QUIZ No. 13 THE FA CUP FINALS OF 1901, 1921, 1981, 1982, 1987 & 1991

1. Cameron, Brown and Smith
2. Ricky Villa
3. Terry Fenwick
4. Bennett
5. Jimmy Dimmock
6. Tommy Hutchison
7. Gary Mabbutt and Paul Allen
8. Glenn Hoddle
9. Steve Sedgley
10. Des Walker

QUIZ No. 14 FOOTBALLER OF THE YEAR

1. Dele Alli
2. Pat Jennings
3. Richard Gough
4. Danny Blanchflower
5. Luka Modric
6. Gary Mabbutt
7. Steve Perryman and Clive Allen
8. Glenn Hoddle

9. Gary Lineker, Jurgen Klinsmann and David Ginola
10. Gareth Bale

QUIZ No. 15 FOREIGN IMPORTS - PART 1

1. Porto
2. Roma
3. Inter Milan
4. Lens
5. Dinamo Zagreb
6. Ajax
7. Borussia Moenchengladbach
8. Twente
9. Estudiantes
10. P.S.G

QUIZ No. 16 FOREIGN IMPORTS - PART 2

1. P.S.V. Eindhoven
2. Bayer Leverkusen
3. Spartak Moscow
4. Real Madrid
5. Hoffenheim
6. Ajax
7. Sporting Lisbon
8. Atletico Madrid
9. Marseilles
10. Lyon

QUIZ No. 17 GOALKEEPERS - PART 1

1. Brad Friedel
2. Bobby Mimms
3. Hans Segers and Neil Sullivan
4. Ted Ditchburn
5. Ian Walker (Leicester's sponsor was Walkers Crisps)
6. Paul Robinson
7. Steve Ogrizovic and Mark Crossley
8. Bill Brown and Roy Brown
9. Espen Baardsen
10. Carlo Cudicini and Frode Grodas

QUIZ No. 18 GOALKEEPERS - PART 2

1. Mark Kendall
2. Erik Thorstvedt
3. One started at Watford and then joined Spurs, while the other went from Spurs to Watford

4. Hugo Lloris
5. Milija Aleksic
6. John Hollowbread
7. Ron Reynolds
8. Kasey Keller
9. Ken Hancock
10. Ray Clemence and Barry Daines

QUIZ No. 19 HOTSPUR HIDINGS

1. Newcastle United
2. Manchester City
3. Birmingham City
4. Blackburn Rovers and Burnley
5. Derby County
6. Liverpool
7. Bolton Wanderers
8. Huddersfield Town and Newcastle United
9. Casuals
10. Old Etonians

QUIZ No. 20 INTERNATIONALS - ENGLAND

1. Peter Crouch
2. Steve Hodge
3. Ralph Coates, two
4. Alf Ramsey
5. Yes
6. Gary Lineker
7. Danny Rose
8. Aaron Lennon and Jake Livermore
9. Walker, Ian and Kyle
10. Jermaine Defoe, Michael Dawson and Eric Dier

QUIZ No. 21 INTERNATIONALS - SCOTLAND, WALES, NORTHERN IRELAND & THE REPUBLIC

1. Dave Mackay
2. Danny Blanchflower, Northern Ireland – 1958
3. Simon Davies
4. Gerry Armstrong
5. West Ham United
6. Bill Brown and Neil Sullivan
7. Colin Calderwood
8. Terry Yorath, Wales
9. Stephen Carr
10. Cliff Jones and Gareth Bale

QUIZ No. 22 INTERNATIONALS – OVERSEAS – PART ONE

1. Ukraine
2. Algeria
3. Denmark
4. South Korea
5. Ivory Coast
6. Bulgaria
7. Argentina
8. Israel
9. Holland
10. Belgium

QUIZ No. 23 INTERNATIONALS – OVERSEAS – PART 2

1. Colombia
2. France
3. Romania
4. Norway
5. Iceland
6. Switzerland
7. Spain
8. Nigeria
9. Kenya
10. Togo

QUIZ No. 24 JOBS FOR THE BOYS

1. Peter Baker
2. George Goldsmith
3. Ledley King
4. Bobby Smith
5. Ben Thatcher
6. Alex Hunter
7. Paul Miller
8. Ryan Mason
9. Albert Page
10. Anthony Gardner

QUIZ No. 25 LEAGUE CUP FINALS

1. Chelsea
2. Manchester United
3. Ralph Coates
4. Ronnie Whelan of Liverpool
5. Allan Nielsen and Kasey Keller
6. Aston Villa
7. Martin Chivers
8. Blackburn Rovers
9. Christian Ziege
10. Jonathan Woodgate

QUIZ No. 26 LONDON LINKS

1. Martin Peters and West Ham United
2. Les Ferdinand and QPR
3. Andros Townsend and Crystal Palace
4. Jimmy Greaves and Chelsea
5. Sol Campbell and Arsenal
6. Scott Parker and Charlton, Chelsea and West Ham United
7. Michael Carrick and West Ham United
8. Darren Bent and Charlton
9. West Ham United
10. Scott Parker

QUIZ No. 27 MAD MATCHES

1. 7-5
2. Wolves
3. 5-5
4. 5-3 to Spurs
5. Huddersfield Town
6. 5-5
7. 6-4 to Spurs
8. Leicester City – 5-4 to Spurs
9. Sheffield Wednesday
10. Burnley and West Ham United

QUIZ No. 28 MANAGERS – PART 1

1. Bill Nicholson
2. Glenn Hoddle, Harry Redknapp and Mauricio Pochettino
3. Osvaldo Ardiles
4. Tim Sherwood
5. Keith Burkinshaw
6. Martin Jol
7. Peter McWilliam, Peter Shreeves and David Pleat
8. Juande Ramos
9. Christian Gross
10. Gerry Francis

QUIZ No. 29 MANAGERS – PART2

1. Jose Mourinho
2. Joe Hulme, George Graham and Terry Neill
3. John Cameron
4. Andre Villas-Boas
5. Arthur Rowe
6. Jack Tresadern

7. Jacques Santini
8. Referee
9. Norwich City
10. Jimmy Anderson

QUIZ No. 30 MULTIPLE CHOICE

1. c – Redknapp
2. d – White
3. a – Chelsea
4. d – Manchester United
5. b – Ray Clemence
6. d – Brighton
7. a – Mike England
8. a – Collar
9. d – Harry Kane
10. a – Eriksen

QUIZ No. 31 NOT SO HOT SPURS! (GIANT KILLING)

1. Swindon Town
2. Reading
3. Norwich City
4. Port Vale
5. York City
6. Bournemouth
7. Norwich City
8. Wrexham
9. Swansea
10. Grimsby Town

QUIZ No. 32 ODD MAN OUT

1. Stephen Carr – he went from Spurs to Newcastle United while the rest went the other way
2. Alan Brazil – he went from Ipswich Town to Spurs while the rest went the other way
3. Tom Carroll – he went from Spurs to Swansea while the rest went the other way
4. Paul Walsh – he went from Spurs to Portsmouth while the rest went the other way
5. Maurice Norman – he went from Norwich to Spurs while the rest went the other way
6. David Howells – he went from Spurs to Southampton while the rest went the other way
7. Paul Allen – he went from Spurs to West Ham United while the rest went the other way

8. Laurie Brown – he went from Arsenal to Spurs while the rest went the other way
9. Arthur Grimsdell – he went from Watford to Spurs while the rest went the other way
10. Paul Stewart – he went from Spurs to Liverpool while the rest went the other way

QUIZ No. 33 ONE CAP WONDERS

1. Harry Clarke
2. Ryan Mason
3. Ron Henry
4. Steve Perryman
5. George Robb
6. Terry Fenwick
7. Arthur Willis
8. Bill Nicholson
9. Anthony Gardner
10. Steven Caulker

QUIZ No. 34 THE 100 CLUB

1. Billy Minter
2. Robbie Keane and Harry Kane
3. Jimmy Greaves and Alan Gilzean
4. Teddy Sheringham
5. Sheffield
6. Bobby Smith
7. Les Bennett and Len Duquemin
8. George Hunt
9. Jermaine Defoe
10. Glenn Hoddle

QUIZ No. 35 SCOTTISH SPURS

1. Aberdeen
2. Dundee
3. Rangers
4. Dundee
5. Dundee
6. Rangers
7. Hearts
8. Morton
9. St. Mirren
10. Falkirk

QUIZ No. 36 SPURS V ARSENAL – ASSORTMENT

1. Gica Popescu
2. Cliff Jones
3. 1990/91
4. John Hendry
5. The Titanic Disaster Fund
6. Darkness
7. It was Spurs 100th goal in the Derby
8. Laurie Brown
9. Chris Hughton
10. He was the first substitute in a Spurs' v Arsenal match

QUIZ No. 37 SPURS V ARSENAL – THE FA CUP

1. The 1940s
2. Six
3. No
4. Garth Crooks
5. Old Trafford
6. Paul Gascoigne and Gary Lineker
7. Gary Doherty
8. George Graham
9. False
10. 1991 – semi-final

QUIZ No. 38 SPURS V ARSENAL – THE LEAGUE 1909-1999

1. 'Taffy' O'Callaghan
2. Terry Dyson
3. Mark Falco
4. Cliff Jones and Chris Jones
5. Les Allen and Clive Allen
6. Micky Hazard, Alan Gilzean, Alan Brazil
7. Willie Young
8. 5-0
9. John Curtis
10. Bobby Smith

QUIZ No. 39 SPURS V ARSENAL – THE LEAGUE 2000-20

1. Kevin Wimmer
2. Ledley King, Freddie Kanoute and Robbie Keane
3. Rafael Van der Vaart
4. One – Harry Kane
5. Nacer Chadli
6. Dimitar Berbatov

7. Darren Anderton, Emmanuel Adebayor, Dele Alli and Toby Alderweireld
8. David Bentley, William Gallas and Emmanuel Adebayor
9. Teddy Sheringham and Louis Saha
10. Rafael Van der Vaart and Harry Kane

QUIZ No. 40 SPURS V ARSENAL – THE LEAGUE CUP

1. Jimmy Greaves
2. Ossie Ardiles
3. Glenn Hoddle
4. Clive Allen
5. Dimitar Berbatov
6. Mido
7. Jermaine Jenas
8. Robbie Keane
9. Calum Chambers
10. Dele Alli and Son

QUIZ No. 41 SPURS IN THE FA CUP – 1894-1939

1. West Herts
2. Luton Town
3. Liverpool
4. Sandy Brown
5. Preston North End
6. Incorrect pitch markings
7. 9-0
8. Bristol Rovers
9. Plymouth Argyle and Watford
10. West Ham United at Highbury

QUIZ No. 42 SPURS IN THE FA CUP – 1946-60

1. Blackpool
2. Leicester City
3. Newport County
4. Len Duquemin
5. Birmingham City
6. Score from the penalty spot
7. West Ham United
8. Les Allen
9. Ted Ditchburn and Ron Reynolds
10. Les Bennett

QUIZ No. 43 SPURS IN CUP COMPETITIONS – THE 1960s

1. Manchester City
2. Chelsea

3. Alan Gilzean
4. Sunderland
5. Jimmy Greaves
6. 5-1
7. Burnley
8. West Ham United
9. Aston Villa
10. Terry Dyson

QUIZ No. 44 SPURS IN CUP COMPETITIONS - THE 1970s

1. Five
2. Leeds United
3. Middlesbrough
4. Bristol City
5. Carlisle United
6. Liverpool
7. Wolves and the UEFA Cup Final of 1972
8. Manchester United
9. Margate and Altrincham and the venue was Maine Road, Manchester
10. Doncaster Rovers

QUIZ No. 45 SPURS IN CUP COMPETITIONS - THE 1980s

1. QPR
2. Bradford City
3. Wolves, Leicester City and Watford
4. Barnsley, Birmingham City and West Ham United
5. 16
6. Garth Crooks
7. Micky Hazard
8. Orient, Crystal Palace, Arsenal and West Ham United. The latter beat Spurs
9. David Howells
10. Steve Hodge

QUIZ No. 46 SPURS IN CUP COMPETITIONS - THE 1990s

1. Arsenal
2. Bolton Wanderers, Fulham and Derby County
3. Paul Gascoigne
4. Watford and Southampton
5. Teddy Sheringham and a bull
6. Marlow and Altrincham
7. Barnsley and David Ginola

8. Brentford
9. Newcastle United
10. Nottingham

QUIZ No. 47 SPURS IN THE FOOTBALL LEAGUE - 1908-39

1. Bolton Wanderers
2. Wolves
3. It was the only time Spurs fielded three brothers in a game. They were Alex, Bobby and Danny Steel
4. Score the first hat-trick by a Spurs player in the Football League
5. 17th
6. Bert Bliss
7. Chelsea
8. Cecil Poynton
9. Everton
10. Stoke City

QUIZ No. 48 SPURS IN THE FOOTBALL LEAGUE - 1946-60

1. Les Bennett
2. Sheffield United
3. Liverpool, Everton, Ipswich Town and Nottingham Forest
4. Stoke City
5. Huddersfield Town and Arsenal
6. Second
7. Six
8. Alfie Stokes
9. Tommy Harmer
10. Wolves

QUIZ No. 49 SPURS IN THE FOOTBALL LEAGUE - THE 1960s

1. Ipswich Town
2. 57 less
3. Upton Park
4. Liverpool
5. Blackburn Rovers and Blackpool
6. Cliff Jones
7. One
8. Peter Rodrigues
9. Burnley
10. Alan Gilzean

QUIZ No. 50 SPURS IN THE FOOTBALL LEAGUE - THE 1970s

1. Martin Chivers, Martin Peters and Steve Perryman

2. Chris Jones
3. They were playing Leeds United, whose Elland Road ground had been closed by the authorities
4. Martin Peters
5. Won 14, Drew 14, Lost 14
6. Alfie Conn
7. Keith Osgood
8. Six
9. Southampton and Brighton
10. They both scored three

QUIZ No. 51 SPURS IN THE FOOTBALL LEAGUE – THE 1980s

1. Garth Crooks
2. Manchester United
3. Wolves
4. Gary Mabbutt
5. Steve Archibald
6. QPR
7. Clive got 33 and Paul got three
8. True
9. Millwall
10. Chris Fairclough

QUIZ No. 52 SPURS IN THE FOOTBALL LEAGUE – THE 1990s

1. Paul Gascoigne
2. Gary Lineker
3. Wimbledon
4. Leeds United
5. Oldham Athletic
6. Jurgen Klinsmann and Sheffield Wednesday
7. Neil Ruddock
8. Chris Armstrong
9. Dean Richards
10. Teddy Sheringham and Ian Walker

QUIZ No. 53 SPURS IN EUROPE – THE 1960s

1. The European Cup
2. Gornik Zabreze
3. 8-1, Cliff Jones
4. Terry Dyson
5. Benfica
6. Glasgow Rangers
7. 5-1
8. Manchester United
9. Dave Mackay
10. Olympique Lyon

QUIZ No. 54 SPURS IN EUROPE – THE 1970s

1. Alan Gilzean and Martin Chivers
2. Martin Peters
3. AC Milan
4. Steve Perryman
5. Alan Mullery
6. Liverpool
7. Grasshoppers
8. Aberdeen
9. Mike England and Feyenoord
10. Hooliganism

QUIZ No. 55 SPURS IN EUROPE – THE 1980s

1. Ajax
2. Dundalk
3. Barcelona
4. Graham Roberts
5. Garth Crooks
6. Chris Hughton
7. 14
8. Benfica
9. Paul Miller
10. Tony Parks

QUIZ No. 56 SPURS IN EUROPE – THE 1990s AND 2000s

1. Feyenoord
2. Gordon Durie
3. Leonhardsen and Perry
4. Berbatov
5. Steed Malbranque
6. Freddie Kanoute
7. Slavia Prague
8. P.S.V. Eindhoven
9. Darren Bent
10. Shakhtar Donetsk

QUIZ No. 57 SPURS IN EUROPE – 2010s – CLUBS

1. Milan
2. Hearts and Shamrock Rovers
3. Lazio
4. Benfica
5. Fiorentina
6. C.S.K.A. Moscow
7. Gent
8. Anderlecht – Europa League Group J – 2015/1
9. Ajax
10. Bayern Munich and RB Leipzig

QUIZ No. 58 SPURS IN EUROPE - 2010s - PLAYERS

1. Peter Crouch
2. Gareth Bale
3. Defoe, Dembele and Dempsey
4. Soldado
5. Eric Lamela
6. Toby Alderweireld
7. Harry Kane
8. Lucas Moura
9. Fernando Llorente
10. Lo Celso, Aurier and Sessegnon

QUIZ No. 59 SPURS IN THE SOUTHERN LEAGUE - 1896-1908

1. a – Chatham
2. c – Gillingham
3. b – 1899–1900
4. d – Watford
5. c – Southampton
6. b – five
7. a – QPR
8. d – David Copeland
9. c – Preston North End
10. b – Vivian Woodward

QUIZ No. 60 SPURS QUOTES

1. Harry Redknapp on William Gallas
2. Graeme Souness to Graham Poll
3. Paul Gascoigne prefers a drink over Glenn Hoddle's faith healer
4. Alan Sugar on Terry Venables
5. Christian Ziege
6. Tim Sherwood on Glenn Hoddle
7. Christian Gross
8. Steve Perryman and Exeter City
9. Terry Venables on Paul Gascoigne's move to Lazio
10. Benoit Assou-Ekotto

QUIZ No. 61 SUPER SPURS - OSVALDO ARDILES

1. Huracan
2. Derby County
3. Manchester United
4. Ajax and Austria Vienna
5. Brighton & Hove Albion
6. He left Spurs due to the Falklands conflict
7. P.S.G. and QPR

8. Swindon Town, West Bromwich Albion and Newcastle United
9. Chas and Dave
10. Martin Peters, Jurgen Klinsmann and Hugo Lloris

QUIZ No. 62 SUPER SPURS - DANNY BLANCHFLOWER

1. Glentoran
2. Barnsley
3. Aston Villa
4. Manchester City
5. Shredded Wheat
6. To equalise before the other team score!
7. The quarter-final
8. Burnley in the FA Cup Final and Benfica in the European Cup semi-final second leg
9. Eamonn Andrews
10. Leeds United and Leicester City

QUIZ No. 63 SUPER SPURS - JIMMY GREAVES

1. He scored at White Hart Lane for Chelsea against Spurs
2. AC Milan
3. £99,999
4. Blackpool
5. Peru
6. 37
7. Eight; Martin Chivers
8. Martin Peters
9. Derby County
10. Vivian Woodward

QUIZ No. 64 SUPER SPURS - GLENN HODDLE

1. Norwich City
2. Stoke City
3. Eintracht Frankfurt
4. Barnsley
5. Bulgaria
6. Coventry City
7. 1979/80
8. QPR
9. Birmingham City and Wrexham
10. Monaco

QUIZ No. 65 SUPER SPURS – PAT JENNINGS

1. Newry Town
2. Watford
3. Bobby Tambling of Chelsea
4. Alex Stepney
5. Peter Shilton and Shay Given
6. Saved two penalties in a 1-1 draw
7. Peter Shilton, Gordon Banks, Bert Trautmann and Neville Southall
8. Ted Ditchburn
9. 758
10. Joe Jordan

QUIZ No. 66 SUPER SPURS – CLIFF JONES

1. Swansea Town and Fulham
2. £35,000
3. Leicester City
4. Mel Hopkins and Mike England
5. Terry Neill
6. Seven
7. Bobby Smith
8. Crewe Alexandra
9. Terry Medwin
10. Schoolteacher

QUIZ No. 67 SUPER SPURS – ROBBIE KEANE

1. Wolves, Coventry City, Leeds United, West Ham United and Aston Villa
2. Craig Bellamy
3. Inter Milan, Celtic and LA Galaxy
4. Glenn Hoddle, from Leeds United for £7 million
5. Wolves
6. Jens Lehmann
7. Six
8. Virgin Trains
9. Teddy Sheringham
10. He scored at least once in internationals in 19 successive seasons

QUIZ No. 68 SUPER SPURS – LEDLEY KING

1. Anfield
2. George Graham
3. Bradford City
4. Shane Long

5. Yes, it was eight
6. Italy at Elland Road
7. Teddy Sheringham
8. Mexico
9. Stockport County
10. Torquay United

QUIZ No. 69 SUPER SPURS – GARY MABBUTT

1. Luton Town
2. Bristol Rovers
3. Bert Turner
4. Crystal Palace and Wimbledon
5. Drogheda United
6. West Germany
7. Yugoslavia
8. John Fashanu
9. Ewood Park
10. Southampton

QUIZ No. 70 SUPER SPURS – DAVE MACKAY

1. Manchester City
2. Manchester United and Preston North End
3. West Ham United
4. Shrewsbury Town
5. Billy Bremner, Terry Venables and Norman Burtenshaw
6. Newcastle United
7. Coventry City
8. Brian Clough and Derby County
9. Tony Book
10. They've won the league title as players and managers

QUIZ No. 71 SUPER SPURS – BILL NICHOLSON

1. Keith Burkinshaw
2. Fulham, QPR and Chelsea
3. Goodison Park
4. One
5. Peter Baker, Danny Blanchflower and Bobby Smith
6. Ron Burgess
7. 'Good players come alive.'
8. Bolton Wanderers and Newcastle United
9. Ted Drake and Alf Ramsey
10. Carlisle United

QUIZ No. 72 SUPER SPURS - STEVE PERRYMAN

1. 655
2. Sunderland
3. Crystal Palace
4. AC Milan
5. Wolves and Sheffield United
6. Stoke City
7. Reykjavik
8. Alan Devonshire
9. Brentford and Oxford United
10. Start

QUIZ No. 73 TERRIFIC TIMES

1. Nottingham Forest
2. Jermaine Defoe
3. It was the call sign on the popular TV police series Highway Patrol
4. 18
5. 9-3 to Spurs
6. Bristol Rovers
7. Southampton
8. Hull City
9. Tranmere Rovers
10. Leicester City and Everton

QUIZ No. 74 TOTTENHAM HOTSPUR - SEASON 2000/01

1. February
2. Chelsea and Leeds United
3. Four
4. Newcastle United
5. Birmingham City, who beat Arsenal in the final
6. Les Ferdinand
7. Steve Carr
8. Sergei Rebrov
9. Leyton Orient, Charlton Athletic and West Ham United
10. Sol Campbell

QUIZ No. 75 TOTTENHAM HOTSPUR - SEASON 2001/02

1. Neil Sullivan
2. Darren Anderton
3. Tranmere Rovers, Bolton Wanderers and Chelsea
4. Christian Ziege
5. He scored 'own goals' against Spurs in both the FA Cup and League Cup

6. Fulham and Chelsea
7. Les Ferdinand
8. Eidur Gudjohnsen and William Gallas
9. Brad Friedel and Tim Sherwood
10. 10 Bolton Wanderers

QUIZ No. 76 TOTTENHAM HOTSPUR - SEASON 2002/03

1. Top half
2. Steed Malbranque
3. Anthony Gardner
4. Chris Perry and Gustavo Poyet
5. Jermaine Jenas
6. Les Ferdinand and Michael Carrick
7. Cardiff City
8. Kasey Keller
9. Simon Davies
10. Robbie Keane

QUIZ No. 77 TOTTENHAM HOTSPUR - 2003/04

1. Glenn Hoddle and David Pleat
2. Stephane Dalmat
3. Helder Postiga
4. Les Ferdinand, Ben Thatcher, Marcus Bent and Gary Doherty own goal
5. Crystal Palace
6. Manchester City
7. Bobby Zamora
8. Middlesbrough
9. Michael Brown
10. Fulham and Charlton Athletic

QUIZ No. 78 TOTTENHAM HOTSPUR - SEASON 2004/05

1. Jacques Santini
2. Jermaine Defoe
3. Timothy Atouba and Noe Pamarot
4. Oldham Athletic, Bolton Wanderers and Burnley
5. Liverpool
6. Newcastle United
7. Danny Murphy
8. Erik Edman
9. Reto Ziegler
10. Stephen Kelly

QUIZ No. 79 TOTTENHAM HOTSPUR - SEASON 2005/06

1. 1989/90
2. West Ham United
3. Lasagnegate
4. Leicester City
5. Grimsby Town
6. Paul Robinson
7. Mido and Stalteri
8. Craven Cottage and St. James' Park
9. Teemu Tainio
10. Darren Bent

QUIZ No. 80 TOTTENHAM HOTSPUR - SEASON 2006/07

1. Dimitar Berbatov
2. Watford
3. Michael Dawson
4. Paul Stalteri
5. Aaron Lennon
6. Southend United
7. MK Dons and Dele Alli
8. Tom Huddlestone
9. Danny Murphy and Scott Parker
10. Calum Davenport

QUIZ NO. 81 TOTTENHAM HOTSPUR - SEASON 2007/08

1. Dimitar Berbatov
2. Nicklas Bendtner
3. Steed Malbranque
4. Darren Bent
5. Gareth Bale
6. Younes Kaboul
7. Four
8. Robbie Keane
9. Martin Jol and Juande Ramos
10. West Ham United and Portsmouth

QUIZ No. 82 TOTTENHAM HOTSPUR - SEASON 2008/09

1. Two
2. Harry Redknapp and Portsmouth
3. Ten and Heurelho Gomes
4. Roman Pavlyuchenko
5. Sunderland
6. Luka Modric
7. Manchester United
8. Fraizer Campbell
9. Paul Robinson and David Bentley
10. Burnley

QUIZ No. 83 TOTTENHAM HOTSPUR - SEASON 2009/10

1. Peter Crouch
2. By winning the 1960/61 title they qualified for the 1961/62 tournament
3. Jermaine Defoe
4. Kyle Walker and Kyle Naughton
5. Benoit Assou-Ekotto and Sebastien Bassong
6. Robbie Keane
7. Niko Kranjcar and Vedran Corluka
8. Leeds United, Bolton Wanderers and Fulham
9. Doncaster Rovers and Preston North End
10. Manchester United beat Ipswich Town, and Leicester City beat Southampton

QUIZ No. 84 TOTTENHAM HOTSPUR - SEASON 2010/11

1. Wigan Athletic – they conceded nine the season before
2. Luka Modric
3. Martin Skrtel
4. Alan Hutton
5. Aston Villa
6. Aaron Lennon
7. Charlton Athletic, Fulham and Arsenal
8. Peter Crouch
9. Sandro
10. Younes Kaboul

QUIZ No. 85 TOTTENHAM HOTSPUR - SEASON 2011/12

1. Because Chelsea won the Champions League
2. 12
3. Emmanuel Adebayor from Manchester City
4. Watford and Stevenage
5. Giovanni Dos Santos
6. Fabrice Muamba, Howard Webb and Kyle Walker
7. Ryan Nelsen
8. Van der Vaart
9. Stoke City
10. Kyle Walker, Scott Parker and Gareth Bale

QUIZ No. 86 TOTTENHAM HOTSPUR – SEASON 2012/13

1. Andre Villas-Boas
2. Real Madrid – £27 million
3. Reading
4. Jurgen Klinsmann
5. Villa Park
6. Clint Dempsey
7. Liverpool
8. Coventry City and Carlisle United
9. Fulham, Martin Jol and Dimitar Berbatov
10. 12

QUIZ No. 87 TOTTENHAM HOTSPUR – SEASON 2013/14

1. Roberto Soldado
2. Vlad Chiriches and Lewis Holtby
3. Tim Sherwood
4. Arsenal and West Ham United
5. 1960/61
6. Nacer Chadli
7. Paulinho
8. Younes Kaboul
9. Sunderland
10. Gylfi Sigurdsson

QUIZ No. 88 TOTTENHAM HOTSPUR – SEASON 2014/15

1. Argentina and Southampton
2. Gary Lineker
3. Sergio Aguero
4. Christian Eriksen
5. Jake Livermore, Sandro and Gylfi Sigurdsson
6. Andros Townsend
7. Kyle Naughton
8. Kyle Walker
9. Ryan Mason
10. Leicester City

QUIZ No. 89 TOTTENHAM HOTSPUR – SEASON 2015/16

1. Six
2. Dele Alli
3. Toby Alderweireld
4. Kieran Trippier
5. It was his birthday
6. Aaron Lennon
7. Crystal Palace
8. Ben Davies and Eric Dier
9. Danny Rose
10. Bournemouth and Harry Kane

QUIZ No. 90 TOTTENHAM HOTSPUR – SEASON 2016/17

1. 1962/63
2. Leicester City and Liverpool
3. 14
4. Nacer Chadli, Younes Kaboul and Wayne Routledge
5. Wycombe Wanderers
6. Fulham and Millwall
7. Gillingham
8. Josh Onomah
9. Dele Alli
10. West Bromwich Albion and Stoke City

QUIZ No. 91 TOTTENHAM HOTSPUR – SEASON 2017/18

1. 1994/95
2. 3-1
3. Moussa Sissoko
4. Liverpool and Manchester United
5. Paulo Gazzaniga
6. Newport County and Swansea City
7. Harry Kane, who made his league debut for Leyton Orient on that ground
8. Serge Aurier
9. Alan Shearer and Teddy Sheringham
10. Fernando Llorente

QUIZ No. 92 TOTTENHAM HOTSPUR – SEASON 2018/19

1. It was the only season in league football that Spurs failed to draw an away game
2. It was his first goal in August in the league for Spurs
3. Juan Foyth
4. Harry Winks and Victor Wanyama
5. Aubameyang
6. Crystal Palace and Chelsea
7. West Ham United and Arsenal
8. Tranmere Rovers and Serge Aurier
9. Watford
10. Bournemouth

QUIZ No. 93 TOTTENHAM HOTSPUR – SEASON 2019/20

1. Mauricio Pochettino
2. Colchester United
3. Norwich City
4. Lo Celso and Lamela
5. West Ham United
6. Burnley
7. Toby Alderweireld
8. Manchester United
9. Bramall Lane and the Vitality Stadium
10. Five

QUIZ No. 94 THE TOTTENHAM HOTSPUR STADIUM

1. Boris Johnson
2. Eric Pickles
3. 62,303
4. Borussia Dortmund
5. Because they were keen to make a perfect replica, and the original had dents in it because Gazza had once used it as a target when firing an air rifle!
6. Inter Milan
7. Crystal Palace
8. Son
9. Antonio of West Ham United
10. Ten years

QUIZ No. 95 'TOTTENHAM TEARAWAYS' – SENDINGS OFF

1. Alan Mullery
2. Tom Huddlestone
3. Justin Edinburgh
4. Willie Young
5. Edgar Davids and Jan Vertonghen
6. Son, who matched Lee Cattermole's record
7. Serge Aurier
8. Adebayor
9. Borussia Dortmund
10. Peter Crouch

QUIZ No. 96 – TRUE OR FALSE PART 1 – ANYTHING GOES

1. True
2. True
3. True
4. False – it has happened twice, against Atletico Madrid and Anderlecht

5. True
6. False – Nottingham Forest have also done so
7. False – Alf Ramsey had done so before him
8. False – Preston North End in 1921 and 1922
9. True
10. True

QUIZ No. 97 TRUE OR FALSE PART 2 – 'THE DOUBLE'

1. False
2. True
3. True
4. False – Leeds United got 67 points in 1968/69
5. False – Burnley didn't lose a league game against them
6. True
7. False – Aston Villa got 128 in that same 1930/31 season
8. True
9. True
10. True

QUIZ No. 98 VENUES

1. Burnden Park, Bolton
2. Rotterdam
3. Elland Road
4. Stamford Bridge
5. Madrid
6. Highbury
7. Old Trafford
8. Old Trafford
9. Villa Park
10. Hillsborough

QUIZ No. 99 WHAT'S IN A NAME?

1. Tom Morris
2. Joe Meek
3. Jimmy Melia
4. Tommy Roe
5. Joe Allen
6. Brian Statham
7. Matt Dillon
8. George Foreman
9. Peter Collins
10. Bill Brown

QUIZ No. 100 WHITE HART LANE

1. Northumberland Park
2. Notts County
3. 748, Tottenham High Road
4. 5-4 to England
5. They were unbeaten at home in those seasons
6. Sunderland
7. Arsenal and Chelsea
8. Wimbledon and Luton Town
9. They were the first and last Spurs scorers on the ground
10. Wayne Rooney

INTRODUCTION QUESTION

The Milk Marketing Board, Coca-Cola, Worthington, Carling And Carabao.